Highways of the West

Sierra Highway

U.S. 395 and El Camino Sierra in California and Nevada

Stephen H. Provost

SIERRA HIGHWAY

Dragon Crown Books 2023

ISBN: 9798859440184

Acknowledgments

Thanks to the California State University, Chico, Meriam Library Special Collections; Jamie Cummins of New Pine Creek Oregon History; and Joel Windmiller of the Lincoln Highway Association for granting permission to use some of the historical images presented in this book.

Highways of the West

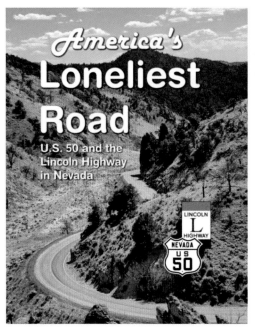

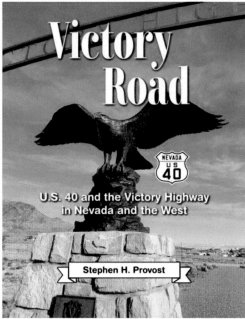

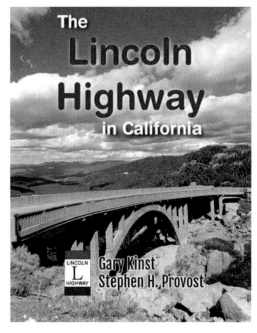

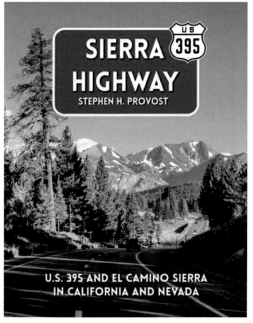

SIERRA HIGHWAY

Contents

Front cover photo by Stephen H. Provost
U.S. Highway 395 between the June Lake
Loop and Mammoth Lakes, looking south

Back cover photo by Stephen H. Provost:
U.S. 395 along the Walker River in Mono
County, north of Bridgeport, looking south

Sierra Highway

SIERRA HIGHWAY

Foreword

By Sharon Marie Provost

When Stephen H. Provost asked me to write this foreword to his book about Highway 395, I readily agreed. It was an absolute delight to do so, for many reasons. First and foremost, it is exciting to give a little personal insight into my love for this highway that has been such a big part of my life, both growing up and now as an adult. Second, it is an honor to introduce the reader to Mr. Provost, now my husband, who is an accomplished journalist/editor with over 30 years of experience and an excellent author of many historical highway volumes.

It is with great enthusiasm that I present this work to you. I hope you will enjoy the adventure along the Sierra Highway as much as I did when my then-fiancé and I researched and traveled along it in preparation for this book.

I was born in Sacramento, California in the late 1970s. When I was ten, my family and I moved to Carson City, Nevada, after my father's job transfer. My sister and I were very excited to see a new city and state. Imagine our astonishment when we were driving on 395 from Reno down the hill into Carson City, and we saw a city so small (compared to Sacramento) that we exclaimed we could "ride our bikes across the city." That drive over the mountains on Interstate 80 from California into Reno, and then down to our new home on U.S. 395, was my first introduction to the highway that would become a major part of my life.

We settled in a house at the south end of town, mere blocks from the so-called "main drag" through town, also known as Carson Street, or more importantly Highway 395.

SIERRA HIGHWAY

There was always a ton of traffic going through town because Nevada is a gambling mecca and, therefore, a major tourist destination. Back then. the road was lined with many small, old motels and old-fashioned drive-in restaurants such as A&W Root Beer and Penguin Ice Cream to cater to the influx of people. However, times changed over the years with the rapid increase in the number of tribal casinos all over the country. The tourism trade slowly died down, and many of those businesses began to disappear—including my beloved Penguin Ice Cream and A&W—as Las Vegas became THE primary destination for tourists.

With those changes in Carson City's tourism came changes to 395. In 2009, Interstate 580 opened as a bypass around the heart of the city. Eventually, the two lanes in each direction on old 395 through town were reduced to one in the downtown area, giving way to wider sidewalks, planter boxes, and parking spaces. The goal was to make downtown friendlier to events such as Wine Walks, The Taste of Downtown, and, most importantly, the capital city's Nevada Day Parade and festivities.

But through it all, Highway 395 held a vital place in my life. It was the main road through town that led to all the stores and restaurants; to my first major volunteering job as a teenager (which evolved into my current career as an office manager at a veterinary hospital); to Reno, where I went shopping at the mall; and to Minden, Gardnerville, and Genoa, with their exciting community fairs and events. When I left high school, I traveled to Juneau, Alaska, for college and then moved to Portland, Oregon for a few years. However, the area of Nevada along Highway 395 remained home in my heart. Needless to say, I ended up back here after a few years.

Shortly after Mr. Provost moved here, he wanted to go on a road trip to explore his new home turf and distract me from my health issues. He wanted to take me to see Mono Lake and the Mammoth Lakes area, which he had visited many years ago. I had heard about these gorgeous Eastern Sierra destinations—plus June Lake, Convict Lake, and the Walker River area—from my grandparents and parents, who had vacationed there many times. My boss also loved that part of the 395 corridor, as well as the area farther south, down to Bishop and Lone Pine.

SIERRA HIGHWAY

Mr. Provost and I began exploring with a day trip to Mono Lake and Mammoth Lakes. It was early spring, so much of the area was still buried in snow, but we were in awe of the beauty we found. This immediately rekindled a desire in Mr. Provost to write a book about the highway, something he'd considered doing many years earlier, but which he never thought would become reality.

We began doing in-depth research on the Eastern Sierra corridor down Highway 395, which led to another trip one month later. The natural beauty of the mountains, forests, and deserts we drove through immediately impressed us. And our fascination only grew as we discovered the Hot Springs Geologic Area, the Alabama Hills (famous as a setting for many movies and TV shows), as well as all the amazing hot springs, waterfalls, and mountain lakes.

At the waterfall above Twin Lakes in Mammoth. *Author photo*

As life became busy and Mr. Provost worked to complete books on the Lincoln and Victory highways, the 395 project was put on hold. But a year later, we decided to head north on 395 and explore where it exits Nevada and continues through California up to the Oregon border. That naturally led us to follow the highway farther south to where it currently ends in Adelanto—and continue on the old routes it once followed all the way down to San Diego's Balboa Park.

I highly encourage you to follow our adventure through California and Nevada on Highway 395. I truly believe there is something for everyone on this road. If you love natural beauty, you will find breathtaking mountain ranges, desolate deserts, colorful hot springs, rushing waterfalls, raging rivers, and alpine lakes.

If you love history, you will find mining towns that have become ghost towns, historic railroad depots, Native American sites, haunted hotels, and the tragic remnants of two World War II-era Japanese internment camps.

Many towns along the way have wonderful museums you will surely enjoy, such as the Lone Pine Film Museum and the Nevada State Railroad Museum in Carson City. You will find crazy roadside attractions or decorations such as the "Hubcap Girl" Uniroyal Gal in Pearsonville; fake ghost town attractions such as the nearby Golden Cactus and Robber's Roost, off 395 near Inyokern; and the Lemon House Inn in Cartago. You are sure to make many precious memories along the way, just as we did.

— Sharon Marie Provost
August 13, 2023

Author's note

I first conceived of a book chronicling the history of U.S. 395 about five years ago as a potential third installment in my *California's Historic Highways* series. Having already written about U.S. 99 and 101, it seemed like an obvious choice. But for various reasons, it never came to fruition. I put it on the back burner, and then life intervened, and I moved to the East Coast.

When I relocated out west again in 2022, Sharon took me on a tour of the highway, reigniting my enthusiasm. After completing books on America's Loneliest Road (U.S. 50 in Nevada), the old Victory Highway, and the Lincoln Highway in California, I decided it was time to resurrect the concept in a new form, along the lines of the approach I'd taken with those three works—with a nod to my California books in the form of the green highway sign on the cover.

Many months of research and exploration went into producing this volume, and I am proud to present the results on the pages ahead.

— Stephen H. Provost
August 24, 2023

A sign in Gardnerville, Nevada, directs motorists along U.S. 395. *Author photo*

Prologue: The Pasear

The highway that runs along the eastern slope of the Sierra Nevada Mountains has a history as colorful as the landscape it follows. As part of the original U.S. highway system founded in 1926, it was intended as a subroute of U.S. 95—which runs just to the east through Winnemucca, Tonopah, and Las Vegas in the heart of Nevada—but despite this, the two highways never actually met.

U.S. 395 wasn't particularly noteworthy back then. In its original form, it covered just a few miles in northeast Washington, taking travelers north into British Columbia. It was only in 1935 that it was extended southward through Oregon all the way to San Diego, becoming the "Three Flags Highway" that ran all the way from the Canadian to the Mexican border.

But the highway's history in California and Nevada goes back much further, long before it was designated as 395. In fact, 395 is just one of several roads that made up what was called El Camino Sierra, part of a projected "great circuit highway" called the Pasear Los Tres Caminos.

True to its name, this scenic loop was envisioned to include two other "caminos" or highways—the more famous El Camino Real along the coast, and the lesser-known Camino Capital from Lake Tahoe to the Bay Area (parts of which were incorporated into the transcontinental Lincoln Highway).

A fourth road, the Camino San Diego north through Riverside, was sometimes included. This would become the section of U.S. 395 that wasn't included in the Sierra Highway.

Of the four roads, only El Camino Real followed (roughly) an old Spanish trail—in this case, connecting the 21 coastal missions on a road marked by more than 400 cast-iron bells. The other two roads were given similar Spanish-sounding names simply as a tool to promote them as romantic, scenic highways at the dawn of the automotive age.

On the highway, 1911

"Briefly, the plan is to join three great highways to complete a circuitous route that would be known as 'The Pasear.' This would include El Camino Real, El Camino Sierra and El Camino Capital... thus closing the circle and making possible a magnificent highway over which automobiles might be driven for a distance of 1500 miles."

— *Berkeley Daily Gazette, December 19*

El Camino Sierra followed the course taken by California Legislative Route 23, which had been established in 1901 as an east-west state highway between Long Barn (east of Sonora) across the Sierra to Bridgeport. Nearly a decade later, this road was extended south from Bridgeport along the eastern slope of the mountains, where it veered west again to Saugus.

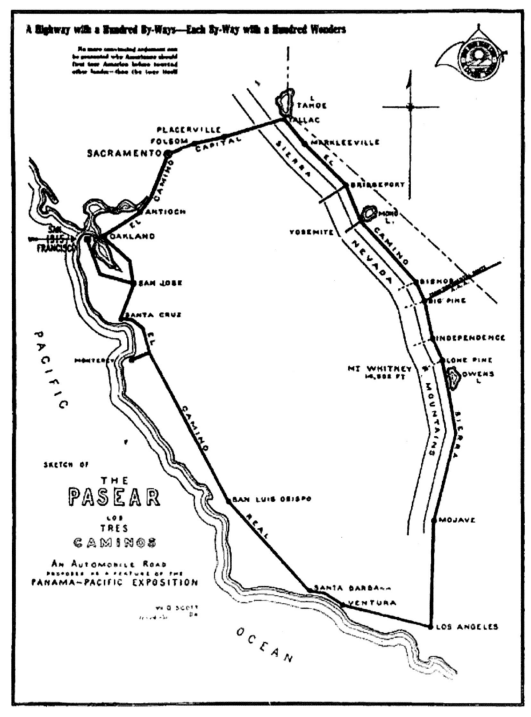

This map of the Pasear Los Tres Caminos appeared in Volume 4 of *American Motorist*, 1912. It omits the southern section of the Pasear Tour, to and from San Diego, which corresponded to modern Interstates 15 and 215. Note that Markleeville and Tallac at Lake Tahoe—neither on modern 395—are included.

In so doing, it funneled travelers into the Los Angeles basin.

A newspaper report on the El Camino Sierra project declared it was feasible precisely because such roads were already in existence: "It would take in a number of roads already in use and in need merely of improvement." This was a common practice for auto trails of the day, which utilized dirt paths, old wagon roads, and railroad rights-of-way to cobble together "highways" between cities and incorporated existing city streets in town.

W. Gillette Scott, secretary of the Inyo Good Road Club, enthused that it would be "a highway with a hundred by-ways, and each by-way with a hundred wonders." Among those wonders: Mount Whitney, Mammoth Lakes, Mono Lake, the Walker River, and Owens Valley.

Scott spearheaded plans to have four Studebaker E-M-F cars set out on a "See America First" tour, intended to demonstrate that the road would be drivable. He dubbed this tour the "Pasear," Spanish for "to stroll" or "to linger," emphasizing its appeal as a leisurely tour for sightseers. He planned to promote it at the 1915 Panama-California Exposition at Balboa Park in San Diego, and he called upon business leaders and residents to come out and line the roads at each of the cities and towns the tour visited.

The Pasear motorists left San Francisco in June of 1912 and traveled down the coast, with stops in places like Santa Cruz, San Luis Obispo, and Ventura, before heading through Los Angeles and reaching their turnaround point in San Diego. From there, they headed back northward through Pasadena and along El Camino Sierra to Lake Tahoe, with drivers passing through Mojave, Bishop, and Bridgeport.

On the highway, 1912

"It is in the El Camino Sierra highway that the greatest interest of the tour is centered. The scenic wonders of this road are said to surpass anything else in California. The road terminates at Tallac on the shores of Lake Tahoe."

— *Berkeley Daily Gazette, December 19*

A Pasear car traverses the Long Valley area. *McCurry Foto*

The *Gardnerville Record-Courier*, just over the state line in Nevada, estimated that some 4,000 Californians would pass through town during the year, their interest piqued by the Pasear. The entire town of Bishop, turned out. Main Street was swathed in red-white-and-blue bunting, and a huge painting with a Good Roads theme hung over the entrance to the Istalia Hotel, where the motorists were staying.

California State Engineer Wilbur F. McClure and AAA executive Percy J. Walker were among those who joined Scott on the 14-man tour, while a *San Francisco Chronicle* correspondent and a photographer from McCurry Foto came along to document the trip.

That didn't mean the road was a highway in the modern sense: far from it. *The Chronicle* reported in 1912 that the road between Lone Pine and Bishop, a distance of some 60 miles, was "generally bad," with the exception of short stretches that ran over fine volcanic rock. And two years later, a couple of L.A.-area travelers reported that the road was covered with fine silk sand and was "practically impassable" between Independence and Carson City—a distance of more than 200 miles.

An automobile is parked on the Camino Sierra during the Pasear tour in Walker River Canyon. *McCurry Foto*

Divergences

In the years following the success of the Pasear, the arrival of the federal highway system, and the funds that went with it, paved the way for improvements—and changes.

SIERRA HIGHWAY

As mentioned earlier, 395 didn't make it to the Sierra until 1935, creating a corridor all the way from British Columbia to near the Mexican border. Hence its name, the "Three Flags Highway."

In California and Nevada, 395 covered about twice the distance that had been traversed by El Camino Sierra, as mapped out for the Pasear—and in some places, the federal highway followed its own path, diverging entirely from the earlier auto trail.

For nearly 130 miles south of Bishop, U.S. 395 was cosigned with U.S. 6 along the former Camino Sierra. But near Inyokern, 395 continued south, while U.S. 6 veered southwest and continued to follow the Camino Sierra route through Mojave and Lancaster to Saugus. That section of highway is still known as the Sierra Highway, although it's no longer U.S. 6.

Main Street in Lancaster, later part of the Sierra Highway, around 1900.
University of Southern California Libraries and California Historical Society

Highway 6, which once went all the way from the East Coast to Long Beach, was truncated in 1964. At that point, everything west of Bishop was transferred to the state of California, and the section from Bishop to Saugus became State Route 14.

U.S. 395, meanwhile, continued south through Ridgecrest and Adelanto to San Bernardino, then all the way to San Diego via Fallbrook and Escondido. But as with U.S. 6, most of that route doesn't exist anymore—at least not as 395: Southward to San Diego, the route was replaced by Interstate 15.

Top: Two Studebakers park on a rocky section of El Camino Sierra overlooking Bishop Creek during the Pasear.

Above: A wagon train on El Camino Sierra, likely near Bridgeport. *McCurry Foto*

Castle Rock overlooking Lake George in Mono County. *McCurry Foto*

Pasear Tour cars crossing a wooden bridge. *Federal Highway Administration*

How to use this book

This book takes the traveler south along U.S. 395 from New Pine Creek at the Oregon state line to its current southern terminus near Victorville. Highway shields will appear along the way to show you where you are. Most of the route is in California, but the section between Reno and Topaz Lake is in Nevada, so shields will appear to reflect that.

State highway shields will appear on significant detours to interesting places off the main route, such as Cedarville, Jess Valley, June Lake, Genoa, and the Alabama Hills. Zero in on any specific destination you'd like.

If you want to follow the road from south to north, simply start at the back and make your way toward the front. Whichever direction you're going, it will take you a full day (10½ hours nonstop) to travel between Oregon and Victorville, a distance of some 630 miles—and that's not counting the section to San Diego included in the Epilogue.

SIERRA HIGHWAY

Itinerary

Continued on next page

A California welcome sign greets motorists traveling south on U.S. 395 at New Pine Creek. *Author photo*

Northern California
New Pine Creek to Nevada   193 miles

The highway between the Oregon state line and Susanville passes through rural land with few inhabitants but plenty of natural beauty. The only town of any size, Alturas, had fewer than 3,000 residents as of 2020, with other communities along the way serving as home to a few dozen inhabitants—if that.

The highway from the small settlement of New Pine Creek at the state line south to Susanville is a mixture of rolling hills and mesas, some of which rest on a prehistoric lava flow. You can see lava rocks dating back 25 million years that have tumbled down the mountainsides in canyons such as the road to Jess Valley, which lies about a dozen miles east of 395 from the town of Lively.

SIERRA HIGHWAY

Wild horses can be seen roaming the Devil's Garden region just west of the highway and north of Alturas. Natural wetlands are home to sandhill cranes, Canada geese, and deer. Signs along State Route 299, which forks eastward toward Nevada just north of town, caution motorists to be alert for pronghorn—the fastest animal in North America—who have a penchant for bounding out onto the road. (U.S. 395 and SR 299 share the same roadway for a brief stretch of about six miles north of Alturas.)

Farther south, heading toward Susanville, 395 passes through an evergreen forest that allows plenty of space for the sun to shine through. Elevations in the general range of 4,500 to 5,500 feet offer a mixture of fir and pine trees and high plains.

In fact, logging was a key industry in the area from the outset, with mills being set up to process tons of timber. Pine logs were first hauled in from nearby to be processed at a water-powered sawmill built by John Bucher in 1867, and other mills quickly sprang up. Within a few years, a mill in Cedar Pass, now on SR 299, was processing 4,000 board feet of lumber a day.

Gold brought earlier settlers to the area via the Applegate Trail south of Goose Lake, which entered the area through Surprise Valley. Some emigrants left the trail at Goose Lake and followed the Pit River southwest into the area that would be home to the modern highway.

Many years later, that highway—U.S. 395—came together piece by piece, running along two former California state roads. Legislative Route 29, created in 1909 as an east-west highway connecting Red Bluff and Susanville, was extended from there on to Reno 10 years later. The segment of 395 between Alturas and the Oregon state line, meanwhile, ran along Legislative Route 73.

That left the area from Alturas to Susanville as rough going.

By early 1929, an improved gravel highway made traveling between Alturas and the little town of Likely relatively smooth, but that section of less than 20 miles was followed by a much longer 85-mile stretch of unimproved road that created difficulties—especially in the winter months—for motorists traveling to Susanville.

Beyond that point, however, drivers could expect "fine traveling" on an "excellent gravel highway" the *Napa Daily Register* reported.

There wasn't much reason to stop. Places like Termo and Ravendale were little more than roadside rests, originally built along the Nevada-California-Oregon Railway line, which started in Reno and followed a northward course along the Sierra, reaching Likely in 1907 and Alturas the following year. Its ultimate terminus became Lakeview, Oregon, after plans for an extension to the Washington state line were never realized.

The company went out of business in 1925 and sold its line to Southern Pacific, which kept it operating until the late 20th century.

One vestige of the railroad's presence endured in Secret Valley north of Litchfield: a brothel—called, appropriately enough, Secret Manor—built to serve Old West railroad workers. If you're looking for adult entertainment, however, you're out of luck. The brothel has long been abandoned, and the rickety two-story building (whose roof has been damaged by a fallen tree) sits empty... except for the ghosts that are rumored to haunt it.

As of 2013, it was still accessible by hiking west of 395 and braving a "no trespassing" sign.

On the highway, 1935

"Travel over the Three Flags Highway in the northern part of California and Nevada has increased 100 percent over last year, according to figures of the State Border Patrol near Reno, G.W. Dow, president of the Highway Association, announced on his return this week from a tour of the Three Flags Highway to its northern terminus in Canada. Similar increases in travel have been noted all along the route, Mr. Dow reported, although exact figures are not available in all localities."

— *Tonopah Daily Bonanza, June 24*

Susanville is the largest city along this stretch of the road, although it isn't actually on 395. You'll need to take a slight detour to get to it, but it's so close it qualifies as a highway town.

Farther south, the highway passes through sparsely populated areas that include a couple of small communities, Milford and Doyle, and past Honey Lake, named for the honeydew produced by aphids in the area. A vestige of prehistoric Lake Lahontan, this shallow lake is dry more often than not, taking the form of an alkali flat. But in wet years (such as 2023, the year this book was written), it's reborn, taking its place alongside the many other lakes that line 395 in the Sierra and providing a wetland haven for migrating geese and ducks by the tens of thousands, along with deer, pronghorn, and even a few fish.

The California Department of Fish and Wildlife oversees a protected wetland area of more than 7,500 acres at Honey Lake.

Lakes along or near U.S. 395

Goose Lake: Oregon-California state line, 147 square miles.

Honey Lake: Lassen County, 86 square miles.

Topaz Lake: California-Nevada state line, 3.75 square miles.

Mono Lake: Mono County, 70.5 square miles.

June Lake Loop: Mono County.

    Grant Lake

    Silver Lake

    Gull Lake

    June Lake

Convict Lake: Mono County, 0.25 square miles.

Crowley Lake (reservoir): Mono County, 8.28 square miles.

Owens Lake: Inyo County, historically 110 square miles before being drained.

New Pine Creek

Thanks to a surveyor's blunder, New Pine Creek straddles the Oregon-California state line near Goose Lake, seen in the distance here from 395. A town of barely 100 people today, it was founded in 1876 and had grown to more than 5,000 residents by 1912, when it had seven saloons—all on the Oregon side because there was no sales tax there. The largest building in town, the two-story High Grade Hotel, was thriving around that time but torn down in 1945. At various times in the 20th century, New Pine Creek featured service stations selling Richfield, Texaco, and 76 gas, a grocer called the Faris Store, and a drive-in called Cooper's (which opened in 1948). where you could get ice cream, milkshakes, sandwiches, and coffee. Those businesses are long since gone. *Author photo*

Finding New Pine Creek

Location: 14 miles south of Lakeview, Oregon; 39 miles north of Alturas
Route: U.S. Highway 395

H.M. and T.M. Fleming operated a mercantile in this old building just north of the state line for a quarter-century beginning in 1909 before selling it to a writer named Henry Wendt, a prominent citizen in town. Alvin Butler purchased the mercantile in 1942 and rechristened it Alvin's Market, which he ran with his son Kelton. Butler's store even had an old-fashioned wood stove that served as a community gathering spot during the winter. It became "Just Stuff" in 1994. *Author photo*

On the highway, 2005

"A few years ago, a car on the California side of State Line Road collided with another vehicle at the intersection of U.S. Highway 395. The crash knocked one of the cars a few feet into Oregon, and authorities there charged the car's driver with drunken driving. An Oregon judge dismissed the case, ruling the driver was in California at the time of the collision."

— *Los Angeles Times, June 26*

The Lake Hotel, top, stood on the northwest corner of the road that would become 395 and State Line Road. Its gables were removed to add space, and its name was changed to the High Grade Hotel during the gold boom of 1912. Above, Fleming Bros. around the same time, now the Just Stuff building. *Photos courtesy of Jamie Cummins, New Pine Creek Oregon History*

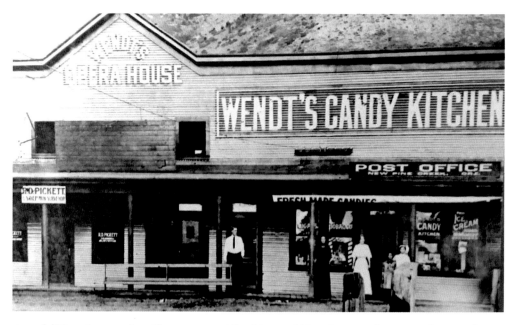

In addition to owning the mercantile, Henry Wendt was the proprietor of a very early "strip mall" in New Pine Creek that included his photography business, a barbershop, the town post office, and the opera house—which doubled as a skating rink, basketball court, movie theater, and pool hall. Then there was Wendt's Candy Kitchen and Ice Cream Parlor. Other mainstays in the community included O.K. Johnson's Texaco service station, which he owned for half a century, and the hotel in the now-abandoned town of Fairport on Goose Lake, which featured a dance pavilion, croquet ground, pier with boat rentals, and swimming pool. It burned in 1930. *Henry Wendt photo, courtesy of Jamie Cummins, New Pine Creek Oregon History*

On the highway, 1934

"When coming through New Pine Creek, remember that you can always find fresh homemade candies. Nearly all flavors of ice cream. Nearly all brands of cigarettes and cigars at Wendt's Candy Kitchen. This week they have pecan crush, cherry marshmallow, maplenut, chocolate, strawberry and vanilla ice cream."

— ***Alturas Plaindealer, June 27***

The High Grade Hotel is seen at the far left in this post-1912 photo. *Photo courtesy of Jamie Cummins, New Pine Creek Oregon History*

On the highway, 1935

"New Pine Creek, the state line town which has been known as the cheapest gas-selling town in this section for several years, dropped gas prices three cents more last week. Johnston Bros., who bought the Sylvester Gallagher Station Nov. 2nd, 1928, have been underselling other towns in this section by three or four cents a gallon. The gas tax in California being 4 cents and in Oregon 6 cents. ... The Oregon-side gas dealers could not compete with them, which left them the only gas station in New Pine Creek until last fall, when Beeson and Heryford bought the lot across the street from their station and started a service station. At the present time, New Pine Creek has a retail gas price[s] of 17 and 19 cents when the regular price in surrounding towns are 24 and 25 cents."

— *Alturas Plaindealer, February 13*

Willow Ranch

Finding Willow Ranch

Location: 1.5 miles west of U.S. 395 on Willow Ranch Road, near the eastern shore of Goose Lake.

No, that's not a space capsule or a giant badminton birdie (above left). It's the burner of the old mill at Willow Ranch, the only element left intact from a once-thriving lumber plant a few miles southwest of New Pine Creek. The plaque at top pays tribute to the "thriving community" built around the "Crane Creek and Willow Ranch lumber companies [that] were [in] operation here from 1929 to 1959." Logs were shipped across Goose Lake to be milled at the plant. The old town store still exists nearby, marked by an old 76 gas sign (see next page).
Author photos

The old Willow Ranch schoolhouse sits abandoned, with a tree growing up through its broken front steps. *Author photo*

The Willow Ranch mercantile store survives on private property just across from the mill site. The once-thriving community included a livery stable, wagon maker, saloon, blacksmith, and carpenter's shop. *Photo courtesy of Jamie Cummins, New Pine Creek Oregon History*

Davis Creek

There isn't much to see in Davis Creek, on the highway about halfway between Oregon and Alturas, but this building is noteworthy. The Davis Creek Mercantile Co. business dates to the 1880s, but it got a new building on the highway in 1952. Two years later, owner Jack Dolan reduced the original building from two floors to a single story. Davis Creek was never large, but it did have a two-story inn (the Hotel Davis Creek), a train depot on the NCO line, and a baseball team that won the county championship in 1896. *Author photo*

On the highway, 1952

"The Davis Creek Mercantile store, owned by Mr. and Mrs. Jack Dolan, opened for business in their new building on the state highway Monday morning with the help of several neighbors. Jack was able to finish moving Sunday. The very attractive building is constructed of pumice brick and is really an addition to Davis Creek."

— *Modoc County Record, April 27*

Top: The two-story version of the Davis Creek Mercantile, probably sometime in the 1920s.

Above: Davis Creek's 1896 baseball team, which claimed the Modoc championship. *California State University, Chico, Meriam Library Special Collections photos*

Like the Davis Creek Mercantile, the Davis Creek Community Church dates back to the 19th century. Founded as the Davis Creek Christian Church, it grew out of a home-based congregation led by Martin Henderson, who purchased the building in 1886 and moved it to its current location just west of the highway. He officiated at the church's first wedding the following year, uniting his own son, Lewis, and his fiancée Minnie Adel Taylor just two weeks into the new year. The pair served as music leader and church organist, respectively. Community events were held at the church over the years, as well as revivals presided over by itinerant preachers. In December of 1938, an evangelist and Assembly of God pastor from Bend, Oregon named D.E. Gribling held meetings that drew "a good many" to the church and proved so popular that the services were scheduled to continue "all this week and perhaps longer." It said so in the *Alturas Plaindealer*, right there on the front page. *Author photo*

Finding Davis Creek

Location: 19 miles south of New Pine Creek; 21 miles north of Alturas

Route: U.S. Highway 395

Top: Motorists turn out to welcome the first Nevada-California-Oregon train to Davis Creek in 1911, as the NCO line expanded northward.

Above: Visitors who arrived by train or car could stay at the Hotel Davis Creek, run by Sam Dutton. *California State University, Chico, Meriam Library Special Collections photos*

Chimney Rock

Chimney Rock is an odd landmark north of Alturas, created when pioneer Thomas Denson settled along the Pit River. By 1871, he had completed a cabin there, which he built beside a rock formation—into which he carved a fireplace and chimney flue. The cabin itself was gone by the 1920s, but the chimney remained, just west of 395 by the railroad tracks. It was the second building Denson constructed in Modoc County, following one at the Dorris Bridge over the Pit River to the south, entering Alturas.
California State University, Chico, Meriam Library Special Collections

Chimney Rock is just one of several rock formations along U.S. 395 about 7 miles north of Alturas, many of them formed from rhyolite ash. *Author photos*

DETOUR Cedarville

In 1867, William T. Cressler and John H. Bonner started Modoc County's first trading post in the building above, two years after it was constructed by James Townsend. It was the first structure built in Cedarville. Unfortunately, Townsend was killed by tribal fighters just after its completion. In 1884, Cressler and Bonner moved into the $18,000 brick building at top, on Main Street, which housed their dry goods, grocery, hardware store, and bank. *Author photos*

Top: Crossing the pass between Alturas and Cedarville in Surprise Valley could be a challenge in winter, as this 1905 photo illustrates. *California State University, Chico, Meriam Library Special Collections*

Above: Once you got to town, if your car needed repairs, you could stop by the Cedarville Garage, which was in business by 1912. *Author photo*

Right: Built in 1938, this building housed a Bank of America branch until 1970 and became a library in 1976. *Author photo*

Grand Opening
SURPRISE VALLEY THEATRE
CEDARVILLE, CALIFORNIA
FRIDAY AND SATURDAY, OCTOBER 18 AND 19
Showing
Love Letters
Starring Joseph Cotten and Jennifer Jones.   News and Shorts
SUNDAY, OCTOBER 20, ONLY
ABBOTT AND COSTELLO in
LITTLE GIANT
Also selected short subjects

Above: Surprise Valley Theatre, above, opened in 1946 with 262 "New Comfort chairs" and stationary projectors. *Granola, cinematreasures, Creative Commons*

Right: Theater building in 2023. *Author photo*

Top: Cedarville Grocery on Main Street at SR 299 was built from local brick for about $8,000 as the Bank of Surprise Valley in 1906. *California State University, Chico, Meriam Library Special Collections*

Above: The bank failed in 1932 and became Kober's Kash and Carry for 40 years before taking on its current name, Cedarville Grocery, seen here in 2023. *Author photo*

Finding Cedarville

Location: 23 miles west of Alturas
Route: State Route 299

Irish immigrant Denis S. Denehy had opened a mercantile by 1901 and was operating in this brick building by 1905. His motto? "Everything for Everybody." That included dry goods, hats, hardware, boots, groceries, canned goods, U.S. Tires, Shell gas, and even Caterpillar and John Deere tractors. D.S. Denehy also had a store in nearby Eagleville, but the company went bankrupt in 1940, eight years after his death. *Author photos*

Cedarville

A and B Market
FRESH AND CURED MEATS

Phone 100   Earl Baker, Mgr.

New Surprise Valley Theatre
Will Open Soon

262 New Comfort chairs — New Stationary
Projectors

The Cedarville Garage
General Repairing   Parts and Accessories

Chevron Gas and R.P.M. Oils

Lenn and Ray Stewart

Kober's Cash Store
Fresh Fruits and Vegetables — Groceries

Phone 201

Cavin's Barber Shop
Ladie's and Gents Haircuttings

Western aGrage
Bailey and Erickson, Props.

Mobil Gas and Oil   General Repairing

Phone 211   Wrecker Service

Valley Service
Chevron Gas and RPM Oil

Ed Ewine — Devern Darnell

Auto Repair   Motor Tune-up

Wylie Pharmacy
Fountain   DRUGS   Liquors

Hotel Golden
MODERN — AIR CONDITIONED

Coffee Shop   Tap Room

T. H. Johnstone
General Merchandise

Hotel Surprise
"A Home Away From Home"

Hotel Surprise Club
NOW OPEN IN NEW LOCATION

Vic and Mac Serving the Best in Liquors and
Mixed Drinks

Pedro's Place
OPENING NEW LOCATION

WEDNESDAY, SEPTEMBER 4

LIQUORS   MIXED DRINKS

"Link" S. Irwin
Wholesale Distributor Standard Oil Products

Surprise Valley

A directory of businesses from *the Modoc County Record* in 1946 showed the town of Cedarville with two garages, a couple of hotels, a movie house, pharmacy, and barber shop, among other businesses.

END DETOUR

47

DETOUR ▶ Tulelake

Tulelake, with its City Hall above, is a small community of about 900 people some 70 miles northwest of Alturas. To get there, take State Route 299 west for 19 miles from the north end of town to Canby, then turn northwest on SR 139 and continue for 49 miles. Tulelake itself isn't much to look at. By itself, it isn't worth a detour, but a couple of stops along the way make the trip one worth considering: the Lava Cave National Monument and the Tule Lake Relocation Camp. *Author photos*

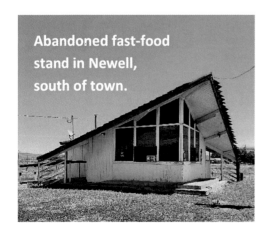

Abandoned fast-food stand in Newell, south of town.

Finding Tulelake

Location: 68 miles northwest of Alturas, past Canby and Lava Caves National Monument
Route: Just off State Route 139

Top: Tulelake has never had many more than 1,000 residents, but its Main Street downtown used to be lined with businesses, including Chevron and Richfield gas stations, a Safeway Market, Marcha Theatre (built c. 1935), soda fountain, and Coffee Cup. All have long since closed, as has the small bowling alley down the block. *Clem Albers, War Relocation Authority*

Above: Closeup of the Safeway in 1939. *Dorothea Lange, Farm Security Administration*

Top: The Homestead Market in Newell, five miles south of Tulelake, had been in business since at least 1948 but was closed in 2023. *Author photo*

Above: The Pastime Café in Tulelake served Coca-Cola and other drinks in 1939. *Dorothea Lange, Farm Security Administration*

Tule Lake Relocation Camp

Top: Overview of the Tule Lake Camp near Newell, one of 10 internment camps run by the War Relocation Authority and the last one to close, on May 5, 1946. Its peak population was nearly 19,000 residents, housed in more than 1,000 barracks and policed by 28 guard towers. *National Park Service*

Above: A Japanese American man leaves a tarpaper-covered barrack housing the Bank of America at Tule Lake Relocation Camp in 1943, *Pete O'Crotty, Library of Congress*

Scenes from the Tule Lake Relocation Center, 1943. The government used it as a segregation center to house Americans of Japanese Ancestry who refused to answer "yes" to a pair of "loyalty" questions:

No. 27: *"Are you willing to serve in the armed forces of the United States on combat duty whenever ordered?"*

No. 28: *"Will you swear unqualified allegiance to the United States of America and faithfully defend the United States from any and all attack by foreign or domestic forces, and foreswear any form of allegiance to the Japanese Emperor or any other foreign government, power, or organization?"*

Pete O'Crotty photos, Library of Congress

Only a handful of buildings remain at the former camp, including the concrete jail, directly above, which was restored at a cost of nearly $400,000 in 2012. When it was operating, the camp included a post office, hospital, factories, cemetery, water wells, chicken and hog farms, and 3,500 acres of farmland. Also within the compound was Castle Rock, an 800-foot bluff that was once an island in prehistoric Tule Lake. A visitor center eight miles south of the city of Tulelake on State Route 139 features displays and literature, and rangers offer guided tours. *Author photos*

Lava Beds National Monument

On your way to Tulelake, stop off at Lava Beds National Monument by taking a 17-mile detour west from State Route 139 at Perez. Some caves can be cold, so wear warm clothing, a helmet, and sturdy footwear, and be sure to take lights— not just a cellphone. The site includes 24 caves, including the Blue Grotto at top and the ice cave at left, some of which have tight crawl spaces. *National Park Service photos*

END DETOUR

The Hotel Niles was built in 1908 as the Curtis Hotel. Jay Eugene Niles, who owned the hotel across the street, purchased it in 1912 and added the second and third floors. *Author photo*

Alturas

County: Modoc *(county seat since 1874)*

Elevation: 6,347

Established: 1870 as Dorris Bridge

Incorporated: 1901

> **1920** — Population: 979
>
> **2020** — Population: 2,715

Key buildings:

> Hotel Niles (1908, expanded 1912)
>
> Modoc County Courthouse (1914)
>
> NCO Railway Building (1917)
>
> Niles Theater (1937)

Alturas, the only incorporated city in Modoc County, was founded around 1870 as Dorris Bridge, named for a bridge built by brothers Presley and James Dorris that spanned the Pit River at the south end of town. They established a trading center there, and a town grew up around it called Dorrisville, but it was renamed Alturas (Spanish for "The Heights") by the Post Office in 1876.

The Dorris family continued to work the land as a livestock ranch for the next 90 years before selling more than 5,000 acres in 1960 to the Bureau of Fisheries and Wildlife, which established the Modoc National Wildlife Refuge there. (Other, smaller tracts of land were purchased over the years, expanding the refuge to more than 7,000 acres. It serves as a migratory stop for ducks, geese, cranes, and other marsh birds on the Pacific Flyway.)

Another name closely associated with Alturas—and still prominently displayed there—is Niles, which has graced the town's historic hotel for more than a century and its theater since the 1930s. Hotels with names like Big Trees, Warner, and Modoc have come and gone, but the Hotel Niles remains, standing alongside U.S. 395 near the south end of town.

J.E. Niles, a Michigan native, traveled across Panama to get to California, settling in Siskiyou County in 1868. He moved to Modoc County and, 20 years later, partnered with Irving Shepherd in the Adin Flour Mills—where he installed Modoc County's first electric light. He added a planing mill at the turn of the century and formed an investment company.

It wasn't until 1908 that he moved to Alturas, where he joined forces with the Laird family to build a two-story building that covered a city block and housed the Niles Hotel.

That building's still there, but it isn't today's hotel.

Today's inn was there, too, but it was just a single story at the time and was known as the Curtis Hotel. Niles purchased it in 1912 and turned it into the new Niles, adding two more floors in the process. He would continue to own the hotel until 1929, when he sold it to new owners who installed the first elevator in Modoc County. (It no longer works; these days, guests take the stairs.)

Top: Main Street in Alturas as it appeared around 1900, more a winding path than a highway.

Above: An S-curve on the road to Alturas, photographed around 1910 when horse-drawn wagons were still a common mode of transportation. *California State University, Chico, Meriam Library Special Collections photos*

But Niles wasn't finished with Alturas. In 1931, he and his son-in-law purchased the town's Alhambra Theatre on Howard Street, built as an opera house in 1897. Six years later, at the age of 84, he built a grander theater to replace it, dubbed the Niles, on the site of an old mercantile. His intention: to provide some encouragement for the town amid the depths of the Great Depression. "I want to prove to the people that things aren't as bad as they seem," he said before construction got underway.

Niles lived another decade before he died at the age of 94 when he was brushed by a car as he stepped off the curb right in front of the theater.

On the highway, 1935

"U.S. Highway No 395 now extends from the Canadian border to Los Angeles via Spokane, Pendleton, Burns, Lakeview, Alturas, Reno, Bishop, Owens Valley and Lancaster. The highway departments of Washington, Oregon, Nevada and California will immediately commence erecting the several thousand signs which will be used to designate the route.

"Obtaining of a federal highway number for the Three Flags Highway comes as a climax of two years of aggressive work by the committees along the route under the able leadership of President George W. Dow, of Lone Pine, Calif., of the Three Flags Highway Association.

"Two years ago the association succeeded in having the California legislature place the Susanville-Alturas 80-mile gap in the California highway system, which stretch of highway was oiled last summer. President Dow personally presented [association's plea for] the federal highway number..."

— *Klamath Falls Evening Herald, December 5*

Author photos

Clockwise from top: The sign over the saloon at the Niles Hotel; an upstairs sitting area; crooked door; and the bridal suite. According to legend, the hotel is haunted by the ghost of a bordello girl who makes a racket by stomping around at night and scratching on the walls, even climbing into bed with male guests (though she doesn't particularly care for them).

Top: The Niles Theatre along 395, looking north, and seen from the front (inset).

Above: J.E. Niles' original hotel, known as the Royal, sat across the street and just down the block from his later Niles Hotel. Now known as the Laird Building, the two-story structure housed a gift shop and restaurant called Wild Mustard as of 2023. *Author photos*

ALHAMBRA THEATRE

ALTURAS, CALIF.
DIRECTION OF EMIL HEBER

Top: The 250-seat Empress Theatre opened downtown in 1913 but was never equipped for sound and was converted into a mercantile building in 1929.

Top photo: California State University, Chico, Meriam Library Special Collections

Above and right: Grand opening ad for the Alhambra in May 1929 in the former opera house. The building has housed Frank's Carpet & Furniture since 1986. *Author photo, right*

From top: The 1934 Veterans Memorial Building, 1879 Auditor-Recorder's Office, and 1900 jailhouse share a park site on the east side of U.S. 395 at the south end of town. A historical marker identifies the site as the Pit River Ford on the Lassen Trail, quoting Elijah Preston Howell in 1849: "We crossed the creek here running between high banks and drove a short distance down the northwest side and encamped."
Author photos

As both the only incorporated city and the seat of Modoc County,
Alturas became home to various government buildings. The county
courthouse (top) on Court Street, was built for $90,000 in 1914, just
two years after the red-brick City Hall (above left) was constructed a
block and a half east of Main/395 on North Street. The adjacent
stone fire station is a 1936 addition. *Author photos*

The railroad got to town before the highway did, with the Nevada-California-Oregon line providing service between Reno and southern Oregon. The "Whistle Stop" depot (top) was built west of its present location in 1906 and moved to its current site on East Street between 3rd and 4th 10 years later, while the NCO administration building (above) was built in 1926 on what would become U.S. 395. It was used as a Navy and Army Air Corps flight training school during World War II and now serves as an Elks Lodge. Passenger service to Alturas ended in 1938. *Author*

The Big Tree Hotel, seen c. 1915 in the photo at top, became the Hotel California 20 years later with all new furniture, mattresses, and linoleum, 18 rooms on the first floor, and a huge fireplace in the lobby. In 1952, a new owner from Sacramento changed the name again: to the Hotel Warner. By this time, the entire façade had been remodeled and the formerly eponymous "big tree": that had once hugged the hotel wall was long gone. The name Warner belongs to a nearby mountain range, which for its part was named in honor of U.S. Army engineer Capt. William H. Warner, who was killed by Native Americans in 1849 while trying to forge a route for a railroad crossing in the Sierra. The Hotel Warner was gone by the 1970s. *California State University, Chico, Meriam Library Special Collections*

Top: A view along U.S. 395, looking north toward the Hotel Modoc, just beyond the Texaco station. Built as the Morse Hotel in the early 1900s, the establishment became the Hotel Modoc in 1912; it was demolished in 1968. *California State University, Chico, Meriam Library Special Collections*

Above: The brick Belli Building, seen at right in the top photo (with the Star Market sign), was built in 1929 at a cost of $39,000. It also housed a Wells Fargo bank and Western Union offices at various times during its history. *Author photo*

Two views looking south on U.S. 395 from similar vantage points show the highway through town as it appeared c. 1945 (top) and in the 1960s (above). Banks and other businesses came and went, but Hart's 5-10-15c store (see 1942 ad, inset) was a constant. Founded in 1934 by Wisconsin native William R. Hart, the store was still operating when the second photo was taken. *California State University, Chico, Meriam Library Special Collections and Wikimedia Commons*

Hart's
5-10-15¢ STORE
Alturas · · California

No rubbing Liquid
Wax pint 25c; qt. 45¢

Red Furniture Polish
10c, 20c, 25c per bottle

Polish Mops—
treated ....39¢

Liquid Shoe Whitening
per bottle........10¢

3-IN-ON-OIL
in cans-bottles ....10¢

Large size .... 25¢

Hotels weren't the only option for staying along the highway in Alturas. Motels were also an option. The Hacienda (above) is still open just north of town, and the Motel Dunes offered "50 Deluxe Rooms" with direct-dial phones, AC and color TV at 511 North Main. You could even eat at a Denny's-style coffee shop called Jerry's next door. *Author photo, author collection*

Finding Alturas

Location: 39 miles south of Oregon,
103 miles north of Susanville
Route: Main Street/U.S. 395

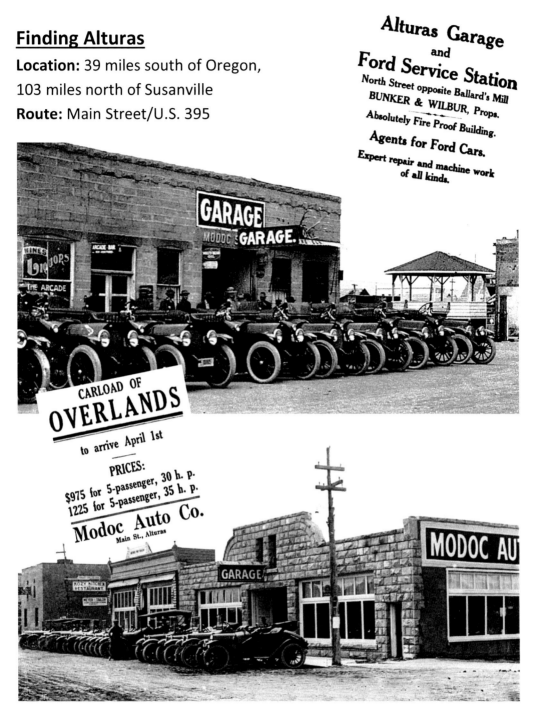

The automobile made its presence felt in Alturas, with the Alturas Garage on North Street and the Modoc Auto Co. on Main competing for business by 1915. (Note Kozy Kitchen Restaurant, Empress Theatre signs at far left, bottom photo.) *California State University, Chico, Meriam Library Special Collections photos*

The lower floor of the original E. Lauer & Sons mercantile building, right, dates to 1876, with the second-floor Masonic Temple added eight years later. E. Lauer moved into its new $200,000 building, above, in 1902, and Sears later operated out of the old E. Lauer location across Carlos Street at Main. E. Lauer stayed in its new 40-by-160-foot "Big Store" —seen at top in 2023 and center in 1915—until 1939. Emanuel Lauer, born in Bavaria in 1831, served as president of the town board and as a county supervisor. He had seven children; his daughter Sara married J.T. Laird, J.E. Niles' early business partner. *California State University, Chico, Meriam Library Special Collections (center) and author photos*

Likely

The Likely General Store is the center of activity in this small highway stop south of Alturas, with a population of 58 as of 2020. Gas is a little more expensive than in Alturas, though, so if you're heading north, you might want to wait to fill up. Heading south, you'd better be sure you have a full tank, because there isn't much between here and Susanville. And if you needed a bathroom break, as of 2023, you had to rely on a porta-potty in the field across from the General Store. *Author photos*

Finding Likely

Location: 19 miles south of Alturas, 88 miles north of Susanville
Route: U.S. 395 at Jess Valley Road

Likely hasn't changed much since this photo was taken back in 1945, but apart from the General Store, you aren't "likely" to find much open. If you're wondering about the name, it wasn't residents' first choice. When they settled there in the 1870s, they wanted to call the place South Fork, after the South Fork of the Pit River. But when the Post Office came to town, officials there nixed the idea, so residents got together at the local store to come up with something better. Unable to reach a consensus, they were about to give up when a stockman named William H. Nelson reportedly said, "Wa'll, it looks as if we're likely to get a name and likely not to." The name was taken as a suggestion, and approved unanimously. It's a Likely story. *California State University, Chico, Meriam Library Special Collections*

On the highway, 1989

"The town consists of the Likely General Store, the Most Likely Café, a little bar, a gas station, an elementary school and not much else. The sidewalks are wooden, which seems appropriate when at day's end the cowboys come into town still wearing spurs that jangle as they make their way up to the saloon. But a new sign has been nailed to the front door of the saloon. It warns that drinking alcoholic beverages can be harmful to pregnant women."

— *San Francisco Examiner, July 9, 1989*

Getting there, 1923

Directions from Alturas south to Susanville, according to the 1923 Automobile Blue Book, with miles between each entry:

0.0 mile: Main & Modoc Sts. South on Main St.

0.3 mile: End of road, left.

0.5 mile: Right-hand road; right.

11.0 miles: End of road; left.

2.0 miles: Thru Likely.

11.7 miles: Fork; left.

1.8 miles: Madeline, fork. Left across RR.

7.2 miles: Pass Brockman Sta.

5.2 miles: Fork; right.

2.6 miles: Termo, beyond RR. Thru diag. 4-cor.

0.9 mile: Fork; left.

1.1 miles: Prom. fork; right; Thru 4-cor.

25.9 miles: Left-hand road; left.

2.0 miles: Fork; left.

1.0 mile: Fork at sawmill; right.

0.3 mile: Fork; right.

2.4 miles: Descend steep, winding grade. Avoid left at foot of grade.

6.4 miles: Left-hand road; left.

0.4 mile: Susanville, 4-cor. (business center two blks. to right). Left.

2.5 miles: Avoid right.

Sign at Likely (with 395 shield), showing miles to Alturas, Susanville. *Author photos*

The Most Likely Café, Likely Garage, and saloon (with phone booth) in 2023. *Author photos*

DETOUR → Jess Valley

Take Jess Valley Road for about 10 miles east of Likely for a scenic treat. It's about a 15-minute drive. When it was first settled, though, it took longer—a lot longer. There wasn't a town in Jess Valley (there still isn't), so residents had to travel to Likely for supplies and provisions. To make the trip in a horse-drawn wagon through canyons strewn with lava rock required at least half a day. A road wasn't cut through the rockslides until 1919, at which point the journey was reduced to about three or four hours. *Author photos*

Finding Jess Valley

Location: About 10 miles east of Likely
Route: Jess Valley Road

The Pit River winds through the canyon alongside Jess Valley Road (below), which is flanked by rockslides like the one at right, made up of lava rock.
Author photos

Only about 10 or 15 families lived in Jess Valley at the dawn of the 20th century, but with six to 12 children each and no way to get across the mountains easily, they needed school of their own. So Orville and Gus Sweeney built this 19-by-32-foot, one-room schoolhouse in 1900. When classes weren't in session, it hosted dances with piano and fiddle music; community dinners and meetings; and church services, before it closed in 1939. The teacher got room and board in addition to pay, staying with one of the families—typically the one with the most children. The school is on the National Register of historic Places. *Author photo*

Life at Jess Valley School

"It was the boys' job to keep the wood box full for the heating stove and the water bucket full for drinking water from the dipper. Each fall, the ranchers would haul wood to school for winter's use. ... When it got real cold in winter, sometimes down to 40 degrees below zero, families would send a chunk of meat as well as go through their cellars for vegetables which the children would bring so the teacher could cook a stew on the flat top heating stove."

— Marion Campbell, former student

Termo

Termo is a ghost town/roadside stop along U.S. 395. Also called Snowstorm and Armstrong, the name "Termo" stems from the fact that it was the original northern terminus of the N.C.O. Railroad back in 1900. When the railroad stopped coming, so did the people. All that remained was the now-abandoned Termo store. There was a post office there from 1900 until 1908 and again from 1915 until the USPS closed it for good, having inspected the building and determined snow and ice on the roof were too much of a danger to patrons, and it might collapse. *Author photos*

Finding Termo

Location: About 45 miles south of Alturas; 58 miles north of Susanville
Route: U.S. 395

The Termo store once sold gas, but it's been a long time, as shown by the state of the pumps, below. A road sign around Lively warns the next gas is 70 miles away in Susanville. *Author photos*

Sulo Lasko bought the general store in 1945 and ran it for some 40 years or more after that. His wife was the postmistress until she died in 1974. In 1983, Lasko still had a stock of 100 faded greeting cards, peanut butter, beer, candy bars, mayo, and three fan belts remaining from 300 he once had on hand. He didn't plan to restock them because there wasn't a market for them: Just 4 people remained in town, even though Lasko charged just $8.33 a month for eight two-room cabins. He also stocked nuts and bolts, but they were free: "People are always in need of a nut or a bolt. I don't sell 'em. I give 'em away."

The 10-unit Ravendale Motel was open in the 1950s but was owned by a church in 2023. You could once make calls from a phone booth across the street, but it now appears to be out of order. Some 62 people lived in Ravendale in 2020. The school closed in 1939 when enrollment dropped to zero, but the California attorney general said the teacher still had to be paid.

Author photos

Finding Ravendale

Location: About 7 miles south of Termo, midway between Alturas and Susanville

Route: U.S. 395

Litchfield

Heard's Market (above), founded in 1948, sold everything from groceries to veterinarian supplies, from health and beauty aids to farrier tools. You could even get "Claude's Country Sausage," in the deli and butcher shop. But Heard's was closed and its sign gone in 2023. Also in town but looking closed: a giant wooden barn labeled "Honey Lake Feed." The 7 Acres Café (below) served "good Basque food" in 1989 but had a burger on its sign in 2023.

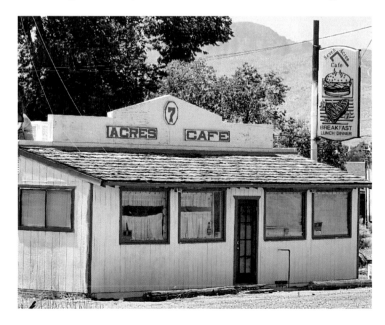

Finding Litchfield

Location: About 15 miles east of Susanville

Route: U.S. 395

Standish

Author photo

Standish Hall was built in 1907 and served as the center for this community, founded in the 1890s and named for Pilgrim leader Miles Standish. Its ground floor housed a mercantile from 1907 to 1954, while the Odd Fellows and other groups met upstairs over the years. Visionary founder William Smythe touted irrigation, with water pumped from Honey Lake, as the key to prosperity in attracting "colonists" to Standish, which had a creamery, canning plant, and other businesses, as well as parks and schools. Pringle Hall, built in 1898, housed a hotel, store, and Bank of Lassen County Branch. It was torn down in 1942.

Finding Standish

Location: About 14 miles east of Susanville; just west of Litchfield
Route: U.S. 395 and Standish-Buntingville Road (County Road A3)

STANDISH MEAT COMPANY
STANDISH, CAL.

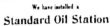

We have installed a **Standard Oil Station** Where we will keep stocked the year round a complete line of Gasoline, Lubricating, Caster and Machine Oils. KEROSENE 5 gallons for **$1.00**

A FULL LINE OF **McCormick Machinery** AND EXTRAS — Practical farmers handle our machinery line. We meet the same troubles and problems that you have to meet. When you come to us get first-class service by men who know just what you need.

BASEBALL DANCE
Benefit L. L. & B. Baseball Team
April 14, 1934

Cindercone Ballroom
STANDISH
... Music by ...
VIRGE'S RHYTHM VENDERS
Novelty Features!
Admission $1.00

A Man Goes to a particular establishment for his first suit on faith, but his second visit is the result of experience. When we sell a suit we rely on that garment to make a permanent customer for this establishment and our hopes have been justified for years. Remember that no sale is complete in this store until you are satisfied.

Kirschbaums Suits For Men $12.50 $15.00 $17.50 $20.00 $22.50 $25.00 and up to $40.00

No Suit On Earth As Good For The Money

EMERSON "Here to Stay"

Standish Meat Co. added Standard Oil pumps in 1917. In '34, the Cindercone Ballroom hosted a benefit "Baseball Dance." The giant log cabin-style structure, built in 1929, had a floor that measured 119-by-50.

In 1916, Emerson's in Standish sold everything from "Food for the family" to "Gas for Lizzie" and "Pills for Dad." Its owner, Charlie Emerson, already had a store in Susanville when he opened a second location in Standish with the motto "Here to Stay." Bill Lewis renamed it the Standish Supply Co. in 1928, and when Claude Heard bought the business and moved to Litchfield, it became Neil's Mercantile.

The Elks Hall was built on land once owned by Susanville founder Isaac Roop and was originally home to a traveling dentist named Jewitt Leonard, who also happened to be a trained architect and built it in 1885. Finding himself in debt, he sold it five years later. Local saloon owner Henry Swain later lived there, and his widow deeded it to the local Elks Lodge in 1931. *Author photo*

Susanville

County: Lassen *(county seat since 1864)*

Elevation: 4,186

Established: 1854 (as Rooptown)

Incorporated: 1900

>**1920** — Population: 918
>
>**2020** — Population: 16,728

Key buildings:

Roop's Fort (1854)

Elks Hall (1885)

Lassen County Court House (1917)

Susanville Railroad Depot (1927)

Sierra Theater (1935)

Susanville isn't technically on U.S. 395 (it's actually about 3 miles east of the highway on State Route 36), but the mileage signs on 395 all point the way to this historic seat of Lassen County.

Founded in 1854 as a trading post by Isaac Roop, who sold whiskey and tobacco alongside food staples, and was originally known as Roop House or Roop's Fort in his honor. A few years later, though, he renamed it Susanville after his daughter.

The community's isolated location put it outside any existing sphere of influence: California to the west and Utah (which then controlled what is now Nevada) far to the east. So 20 local residents met at Roop's Fort and declared their own independent territory called Nataqua, encompassing most of northwestern Nevada, with Peter Lassen as president and Roop as secretary.

The movement added momentum to Nevada's efforts to separate itself from Utah, and in 1859, Roop was named governor of a "provisional territorial government" for Nevada. After Congress officially created the territory two years later, Nataqua was renamed Roop County.

There was just one thorny issue left unresolved: Officials in Plumas County, California, believed Susanville was under their jurisdiction and, therefore, owed them tax money. In 1863, Plumas leaders issued warrants for the arrest of Roop and other leading citizens, sending the sheriff and 40 other men to impose their will on the separatists—who barricaded themselves inside Roop's Fort (aka Fort Defiance).

The two sides began firing shots at each other in a four-hour "war" that left a couple of people injured before cooler heads prevailed and agreed to let California and the Nevada Territory resolve the issue. A survey done shortly afterward confirmed that Susanville was in California, but Plumas County didn't get the last laugh—or those tax dollars. Instead, Susanville was named the seat of a new county, Lassen.

Above: Roop's Fort in 2023. *Author photo*

Right: The fort as it appeared nearly a century earlier, in 1925. *Historic American Buildings Survey*

Susanville's Main Street in the 1940s, with the Mt. Lassen Hotel in the foreground. The $200,000 hotel opened in 1926, having been financed, according to the press, "by the citizens of community and the surrounding territory subscribing to the stock." *California State University, Chico, Meriam Library Special Collections*

Finding Susanville

Location: 104 miles south of Alturas; about 69 miles northwest of Nevada state line and 86 miles northwest of Reno

Coming to Susanville

By the Solicitation of Many Friends and Patients

👁 Dr. H. Ehrlich 💲

The well known **German Eye, Ear, Nose and Throat Surgeon.** from San Francisco, who has been visiting this county for years, and successfully cured by his latest painless methods the most stubborn Eye, Ear, Nose and Throat Troubles, will make his next visit to

SUSANVILLE

Monday, August 6 to Friday; August 20, inclusive EMERSON HOTEL, 8 a. to 8 p. m. Write to Your Friends and Go Early as His Parlors Are Always Crowded

Above: Charles Emerson built the Emerson Hotel at Main and South Lassen streets after his hardware store burned in 1900. The 28,000-square foot hotel included space for his new store, along with a ballroom, restaurant, and 76 guest rooms. But fire seemed to follow Emerson: His hotel was damaged badly in a 1912 blaze and destroyed in another fire three years later. Unfortunately, he was insured for less than half its $200,000 value and didn't have the cash to rebuild. But he did manage to help spearhead the effort to build a new hotel on that site: the Mt. Lassen Hotel. *California State University, Chico, Meriam Library Special Collections*

Left: A newspaper ad for an eye, ear, nose, and throat surgeon scheduled to appear at the hotel Aug. 6-20, 1915. But he never got the chance: the Emerson burned down on Aug. 5, a day before his scheduled premiere.

The now-closed Mt. Lassen Hotel on Main Street opened to great fanfare in the spring of 1926. The $200,000 hotel included 70 bedrooms—each about 12 by 14 feet and most with private baths—main and private dining rooms, and electric lighting in the lobby that gave off an antique gold effect. It housed ice cream and confectionary shops, and offices for a real estate company and AAA. Designed by prolific Nevada architect Frederic DeLongchamps, the Mt. Lassen was under the direction of Frank Coffin, who had previously managed hotels in Redding and Hazen, Nevada. His macabre surname turned out to be sadly prolific: In 1998, the body of another hotel manager, Jack Shepherd, was found wrapped in bloody blankets in his room there. About $900 was found missing from the hotel cash box, and Shepherd's key was missing. Guests have reported hearing what they claim to be disembodied footsteps and Shepherd's ghostly voice echoing in some of the rooms. *Author photo*

Left: The Masonic Temple, like the Mt. Lassen Hotel, has endured since the 1920s and is situated on Lassen Street, like the old hotel. T.J. Rees of Reno was the contractor for both buildings, with the temple being built from locally quarried stone.
Author photo

Above: One historical building that hasn't survived to the present day was the Lassen Industrial Bank building at Main and Gay streets. The bank built the imposing structure in 1922, but Bank of America acquired it in 1928 and demolished it, here, in 1971 after building a new building (seen at far left).
California State University, Chico, Meriam Library Special Collections

The Grand and Pioneer Cafés sit side-by-side on Main Street. Kwan Wong opened The Grand way back in 1909 at the rear of the Pioneer, and it moved to the new two-story building next door three years later. But this isn't the original building: That one collapsed in 1934 thanks to construction work being done next door.

The Pioneer Café is even older than the Grand. A saloon originally known as the Humboldt Exchange opened on the site in 1862 and changed its name to the Pioneer a year later. *Author photos*

This passenger depot, built in 1927, was an addition to the original railroad station built in 1913. Unfortunately, the older structure was destroyed in a 1989 fire, leaving only the historic depot at 431 Richmond Road standing. Southern Pacific closed the depot in 1956, and it was used for storage until renovation efforts began in 1993.

The Lassen County Jail, above left, was built in 1911 and condemned in 1971. The 1917 courthouse, above right, replaced the original 1867 structure— a two-story wood-frame building on the same Lassen Street site. The 2012 Hall of Justice on Riverside Drive is at right. *Author photos*

The Sierra Theatre, built on the site of the old Liberty Theatre, features its original 30-foot-high sign. It opened its doors in 1935 with a showing of Edward G. Robinson in "The Whole Town's Talking." Seats were 35 cents for adults, a

quarter for students, and a dime for children. The theater remained open in 2023. Its predecessor on Main Street, the Liberty, opened in 1921 and was condemned in 1935. *Author photo, top; cinematreasures.com c. 1940s, right*

A Fruit Growers Supply Co. crew poses in the 1930s at the Susanville plant, a lumber mill that made boxes to ship the company's product: Sunkist oranges and other citrus products harvested by the California Fruit Exchange. At one time, the mill employed 1,000 workers and, by 1941, the exchange needed 43 million boxes a year. Extra shifts were added at the Susanville mill to meet the demand. In the early 1950s, however, the exchange (which formally changed its name to Sunkist Growers around the same time) began using cardboard boxes instead. Without further demand for wood boxes, the mill eventually closed. *California State University, Chico, Meriam Library Special Collections*

Above: The Milford Country Store had a minimart and gas station, along with an RV park, on 395 overlooking Honey Lake. It was established in 1894 but was closed when this photo was taken in 2022. At various times, the store sold ARCO gas, submarine sandwiches, and even 8-track tapes: a 1972 ad in the Lassen Advocate touted "Christmas Albums, top rock, country-western, many twin pack and double albums. All for the Low Price of $3.95."

Below: What appears to be an old wigwam-themed motel sits neglected off the old highway. *Author photos*

Finding Milford

Location: 23 miles south of Susanville; 18 miles north of Doyle
Route: U.S. 395, across the highway from Honey Lake

Above: Honey Lake (seen here in 2023), lies on the east side of 395, opposite the Milford with its population of about 150. Honey Lake, a remnant of prehistoric Lake Lahontan, is a shallow lake typically no deeper than 10 feet and sometimes goes completely dry, as it did in 1903 and again from 1917 to 1937. It's a migratory stop for thousands of geese and ducks. *Author photo*

Left: Honey Lake, satellite view. *NASA*

Doyle

The Doyle Grocery & Hotel sits on the north end of town at Main and 3rd streets, just off the Doyle Loop, where the "lizard xing" sign at right was posted. Doyle, with a population of about 500, lost 333 homes to fire in July 2021. *Author photos*

Finding Doyle

Location: About 18 miles south of Milford and 41 miles south of Susanville; 28 miles north of Nevada state line

Route: Doyle Loop, just west of U.S. 395

Getting there, 1923

Directions from Susanville to Reno, according to the 1923 Automobile Blue Book, with miles between each entry:

4.7 miles: Johnstonville, fork at P.O. Left at fork just beyond keep right.

3.7 miles: Fork; left.

4.0 miles: Lassen, at P.O. Keep ahead.

0.7 mile: Fork; right.

1.0 mile: Fork of three roads; take middle road, following poles.

0.5 mile: Buntingville, end of road. Right, avoiding left at P.O. beyond.

9.9 miles: Thru Milford.

1.6 miles: Fork at farm; left.

16.5 miles: Avoid left at outskirts of Doyle.

6.8 miles: Fork at church; left.

0.4 mile: Constantia, Cal., right hand road beyond RR. Right.

The Midway Motel in Doyle.
Author photo

11.4 miles: Left-hand road; left.

3.3 miles: Fork beyond corral; left.

1.2 miles: Fork at fence; right. Sharp right leads to Sierraville and Quincy.

9.8 miles: Left hand road; left across RR.

16.6 miles: Commercial St., beyond RR; left.

0.1 mile: Virginia St.; right.

Bordertown Casino and RV Resort has long welcomed visitors from California heading south toward Reno at Cold Springs, about 15 miles north of Reno. At right, a modern welcome sign stands out at the Bordertown offramp. *Author photos*

Nevada

State line to Topaz Lake

85 miles

The section of U.S. 395 that passes through the Silver State is relatively short compared to the stretches of road in California, but it's no less historic. In fact, the highway in Nevada passes through two of the three largest (and three of the six largest) cities on the current 395.

With the exceptions of Victorville, Adelanto, and Susanville, no California city on the current 395 is as large as Reno, Carson City, or Gardnerville in Nevada.

That wasn't always the case: 395 once continued south through major California hubs like Riverside and San Diego. But since 1969, it's been truncated—and replaced by the interstate system—in the high desert before it reached as far south as the first of big cities, San Bernardino. (Victorville and Adelanto are right at the southern end of the current 395.)

It never was the Sierra Highway down south, which is another reason it isn't included in the main section of this book. Instead, old 395 in Southern California is covered in just a little less detail as an extended epilogue.

Unlike the Southern California section, 395 hasn't disappeared in the metropolitan areas of northwestern Nevada. Instead, through nearly half of its length there, it shares a new road called Interstate 580 for roughly 35 miles from the heart of Reno south to the southern end of Carson City. The last section of this freeway wasn't completed until the summer of 2012, when the Galena Creek Bridge opened in Washoe Valley south of Reno.

Another difference from the Southern California section: Old 395 is still marked here, running parallel to I-580 in northwestern Nevada as an officially signed Business route (in Reno and Carson City) or Alternate route (through the Washoe Valley). So you can still travel old 395 all the way through Nevada if you're so inclined.

When you do, you're covering the same ground once traversed by the old Lincoln Highway, the nation's first transcontinental road, which entered Reno from the east and turned south at Virginia Street—the city's main north-south thoroughfare—and followed what would become U.S. 395 south all the way into Carson City before veering westward again. This makes 395 notable among U.S. federal highways for having shared the road with the two most iconic roads in the nation's history: the Lincoln and, in San Bernardino Couty, Route 66.

South of Carson City, the highway passes the historic town of Genoa—Nevada's first permanent settlement—about four miles to the west as it crosses the Carson Valley. Oddly, Carson City isn't in the valley that shares its name (both having been named for pioneering explorer Kit Carson), but Carson Valley is instead located next door in Douglas County, one of Nevada's original nine counties created by the territorial legislature back in 1891.

The Galena Creek Bridge in Washoe Valley is the largest cathedral arch bridge in the world with a total length of 1,725 feet. *Author photo*

By the time you get to the adjacent towns of Minden and Gardnerville, 395 is a far cry from any interstate. Instead, it's slow going through both towns, where the speed limit is 25, giving you plenty of time to survey the many historic buildings that line the road before heading south and back into California again at beautiful Topaz Lake.

Reno from the air in the late spring of 2023. *Author photo*

Reno

County: Washoe *(county seat since 1871)*

Elevation: 4,186

Established: 1868

Incorporated: 1903

> **1920** — Population: 12,016 (largest in Nevada)
>
> **2020** — Population: 264,165

Key buildings on 395:

> Washoe County Courthouse (1911)
>
> Club Cal-Neva (1914)
>
> Little Waldorf Saloon (1922)
>
> Piggly Wiggly (1926)

Merry Wink Motel (1942)

Landrum's Diner (1947)

Ho-Hum Motel (1953)

Thunderbird Motel (1958)

Virginian Motor Lodge (1960)

777 Motel (1964)

Pioneer Center (1967)

Atlantis Casino Resort Spa (1972)

Magic Carpet Golf (1974)

Circus Circus (1978)

The Virginia Street Bridge carries Old U.S. 395 across the Truckee River, with the 1927 Riverside Hotel at left. *Author photo*

Reno was, in many ways, the city that George Wingfield built. It was already the biggest city in Nevada when Wingfield arrived from Goldfield, where he'd first made his fortune in mining. But it was in Reno where he really came into his own, transforming it into a destination for divorce and (of course) gambling.

Wingfield, who controlled the majority of Nevada's banking assets at the dawn of the Great Depression, left his mark on Reno. Wingfield Park sits on an island in the Truckee River just a couple of blocks west of Virginia Street (Business 395).

Wingfield had already gotten into the hotel business in Goldfield, where he owned the Goldfield Hotel, but when he moved to Reno in 1909, he became even more heavily involved in the "hospitality" game. His bank had supplied Frank Golden with part of the money he needed to build his Golden Hotel—just one block east of future 395—two years earlier, so when Golden died in 1915, Wingfield took over.

That same year, Wingfield built his Reno National Bank at 206 North Virginia Street. The building, which later became part of the now-closed Harrah's hotel-casino complex, still stands on Business 395.

George Wingfield's Reno National Bank as it appeared in 1921, six years after it was built.

Reno National Bank as it appears today. *Author photo*

Wingfield wasn't done, though. In 1927, he built another hotel, the Riverside, at the south end of the Virginia Street Bridge. It wasn't the first hotel by that name along the Truckee River in Reno. In fact, city founder Myron Lake had built his Lake House on the site in 1861, which he replaced with a new wood-frame hotel seven years later after the original burned down. This building, in turn, was rechristened the Riverside in 1888 by Lake's son-in-law, who took over operations after Lake's death.

Harry Gosse of Virginia City replaced that building with a new, four-story brick hotel in 1906, but it, too, burned in 1922. Gosse couldn't afford to rebuild, so he sold the lot to Wingfield, who hired Reno architect Frederic DeLongchamps to design a new six-story hotel on the site. You might recognize DeLongchamps as the architect of the Mt. Lassen Hotel in Susanville. Wingfield knew him well, having previously hired him to design the Reno National Bank building just down the street.

Wingfield now owned the two most prominent hotels in Reno and two-thirds of what would eventually be known as the "Big Three" when the 12-story Mapes Hotel was built within shouting distance of the Riverside on Virginia Street in 1947.

The Mapes Hotel at 10 North Virginia Street was, for a time, the tallest building in Nevada. Its Sky Room played host to the likes of Milton Berle, Sammy Davis Jr., Jimmy Durante, and Frank Sinatra. *Historic American Engineering Record*

Wingfield needed to fill all those rooms, and the advent of the Great Depression made doing so that much more challenging. So he championed a pair of groundbreaking initiatives that would change the face of not only Reno but the entire state. The first was the six-week "quickie divorce," which drew tourists and filled hotel rooms (some entrepreneurs even built motels specifically catering to the divorce crowd). The second was legalized gambling, which was slower to take hold but eventually attracted even more visitors to the state.

Both initiatives passed in 1931, but unfortunately for Wingfield—who owned a dozen banks and controlled more than half of the state's deposits—he was found to have embezzled $500,000 in state money. He was able to pay back the money he owed, but even with his extensive assets, he had to go bankrupt to do so.

Top: The early 20th century chalet-style version of the Riverside Hotel, across from the Carnegie Library, at left. *Author collection*

Above: The Riverside Hotel in 2022. *Author photo*

How did Wingfield deal with such a momentous setback? He simply went back to square one: mining. He'd first struck it rich at Goldfield Consolidated Mines; this time, he accepted an invitation from his friend, state Senator Noble Getchell, to help him develop a new mine near Golconda. The investment proved so successful that, by 1941, the Getchell Mine was producing more gold than any other in the state.

Wingfield sold the Golden Hotel in the 1940s to expand the Riverside and keep it competitive with the newly constructed Mapes. He eventually sold the Riverside in 1955, four years before his death. The Riverside still stands today, but the other two hotels are gone: The Golden burned to the ground in 1962, and the Mapes closed two decades later. Preservation efforts failed, and the building was demolished in 2000.

George Wingfield's home in Reno, at 219 Court Street, was built in 1912 but burned down in 2001.

In addition to the Big Three, there were other hotels in Reno—some of them older and, at one time, with reputations of their own. One such hotel was the Overland, which stood a block over from Virginia Street on Central and dated back to 1903.

Like many early hotels, the Overland—on the southeast corner of Center Street and Commercial Row—was built to provide convenient access to the dominant form of transportation in its day: the railroad. An ad in the Automobile Blue Book 20 years after it was built (seen below) still boasted that it was "opposite [the] depot."

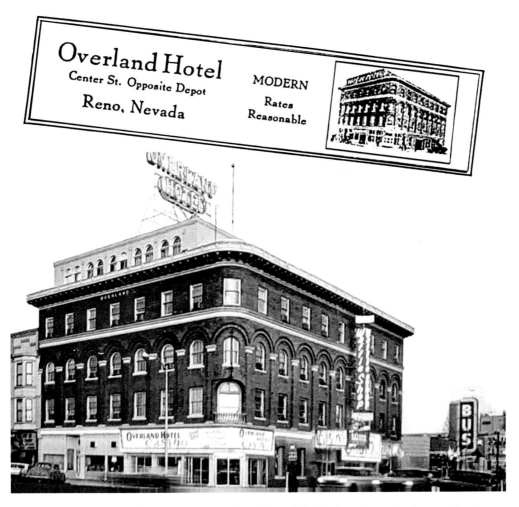

A vintage postcard shows the Overland Hotel in its heyday. *Author collection*

The Overland lasted until 1977, when it was abruptly sold to Harrah's, which demolished the old hotel in favor of a parking lot. (Harrah's itself, seen below in 2022 author photo—shuttered with a labelscar of its name on the side—would close for good in 2020.)

Another early hotel, this one on Virginia Street itself before it became 395, was the Grand Central. Built all the way back in the 19ᵗʰ century at Virginia and Plaza. Dan O'Keefe, its first owner with his brother Tim, built the hotel to replace the Pacific House, which burned to the ground in 1879.

The Grand Central was condemned in 1948 and demolished a year later, but it retains a colorful place in Reno's history. The Irish brothers who owned the place boasted there was "a fight every afternoon at four." This was actually the hotel's motto, referring not to an actual fight, but a daily soccer game. Dan O'Keefe was also a baseball enthusiast: In 1893, he managed a champion Reno team that played its games on vacant lots later occupied by the Nevada Packing Company plant. O'Keefe's boys went unbeaten against teams from Sacramento, Truckee, Virginia City, the University of Nevada, Carson City, Winnemucca, a rival Reno nine, and two other teams.

Still, the Grand Central had a reputation as a rowdy place—and a dangerous one for a certain Louis Bravo, alias "Ortiz," who happened to be staying there in 1891. The *Reno Evening Gazette* described the 27-year-old from Tucson as a "'bold bad man" whose past life "had been one of crime, lawlessness and dissipation" with "not a clean page in it."

After he allegedly beat a man over the head and cut off his ear, Ortiz was fined $75 and, when his friends paid it, freed on the understanding that he was to leave town and never show his face in Reno again. But two months later he was back, drinking himself into a violent fit at the Grand Central, where he began shooting the place up.

He was arrested, but the locals had had enough. Not content with leaving him in jail, about 100 armed vigilantes, disguised with handkerchiefs over their faces, pulled him out of his cell and marched him to the Virginia Street Bridge. There he was given a drink of water and a shot of whiskey before his captors bound him hand and foot, then threw a rope over a crossbeam on the bridge and hanged him until he expired.

He was the first and last person known to have been lynched in Reno.

The El Dorado Resort Casino (1973), Circus Circus Reno (1978), and Silver Legacy (1995) are more recent additions to Virginia Street, Reno's less extensive answer to the Las Vegas Strip. Circus Circus was originally a Grey Reid department store, which opened in 1957. Grey Reid planned its own hotel-casino, the logging-themed "Camp 14," there in 1977 before moving to the Old Town Mall and selling the building. *Author photos*

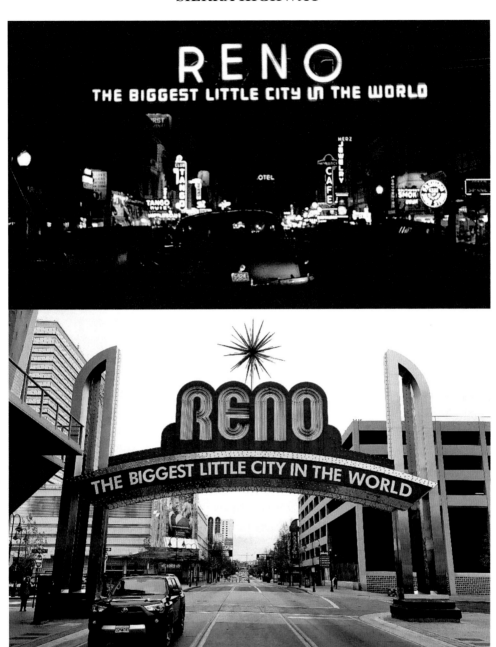

Top: The old Reno Arch, spanning Virginia Street, in 1944. It was installed to commemorate the completion of the Lincoln and Victory Highways at the Nevada Transcontinental Highway Expo in 1926 and has been on display since 1995 on Lake Street south of the Truckee River. *Office of War Information*

Above: The current arch, installed in 1987, replaced a second version, which went up in 1963 and was later moved to Willits, California. *Author photo*

Above: The Nevada Club, promoted in this 1952 newspaper ad, opened in 1946 on Virginia Street downtown. It closed in 1997 and was demolished two years later.

Left: The Horseshoe Casino at 229 North Virginia Street opened in late October 1956 and was a downtown fixture until it closed in 1995. Onetime Reno mayor Bob Cashell was one of its owners. *Author photo*

Top: A closer look at the 1904 Reno Carnegie Library building at Virginia and Mill streets, seen in the postcard on Page 107. By 1930, it had become too small to house the library's collection, which was moved to the Nevada State Building. The vacant Carnegie building was torn down in 1931, and was replaced by a post office in 1934. *Wikimedia Commons*

Above: The post office, with the Riverside Hotel at left. *Author photo*

Left: Their eponymous 12-story hotel-casino wasn't the only building the Mapes family put up along U.S. 395/Virginia Street. They also built this big, boxy structure at the corner of First Street in 1965 to house an F.W. Woolworth store in the basement and bottom two floors, along with offices upstairs.
Author photos

Above: The building in all its glory on a vintage postcard. It wasn't the first location for Woolworth's in Reno: The company had arrived in 1912, opening a much smaller store at 136 Virginia Street. The new store was 40,000 square feet and included a restaurant called the Frontier Room. It stayed open until the chain folded in 1997.

The Little Waldorf, Reno's oldest continuously operating saloon, opened in 1922 at 343 North Virginia Street as a speakeasy during Prohibition, with a 22-foot oak bar in the back room for "members only." It moved to its current location, at 1661 North Virginia, near the University of Nevada-Reno in 1981 after less than a decade at location No. 2, on Fifth Street. In the mid-1990s, it hosted concerts by Bush and Sublime. *Author photos*

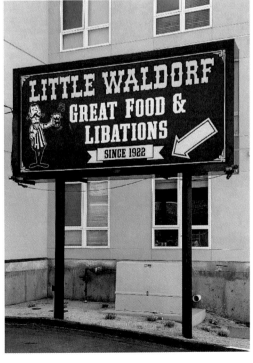

Above: The Washoe County Courthouse began as a red brick building in 1871 on an acre of land donated by Myron C. Lake—who built the forerunner of the Riverside Hotel next door. That structure was incorporated into the new courthouse, completed in 1911 and designed by Frederic DeLongchamps. He also designed additions made in 1946, 1949, and 1963. During the 1930s, more than 33,000 divorces were granted at the courthouse. *Author photos*

Right: The Pioneer Center for the Performing Arts opened in 1967 and featured a striking golden geodesic dome with 500 panels. The statue in this photo, titled "Humanity," was installed in 1939 at the old State Building, which was torn down to make way for the theater.

The Cal-Neva Casino opened in 1948, but part of the building dates to 1914, when it was built as the new home for a department store called Palace Dry Goods House, which opened in another location in 1895. In 1937, it became a casino called Club Fortune, where Sammy Davis Jr. made his Reno debut.

Author photos

Barnes Radio Service, right, opened in a new brick building at 888 South Virginia in 1940. The Giraudo Building, center, at 745 South Virginia housed Gunter's Grocery when it opened in 1928, and Penguin Ice Cream reportedly served 4,500 customers in its first week when it opened there in 1935. *Author photos*

Memphis-based Piggly Wiggly, an early self-service corner grocer, opened its second Reno store in 1926 next door to the Giraudo Building. The market, right, became Sewell's in 1936 and, later, Mount Rose Market.

Right: The Virginian Motor Lodge, built around 1960 near downtown at 500 South Virginia, has one of the tallest signs on the street, surmounted with an old-fashioned-looking faux lantern.

Left: The Sewell family, who had previously taken over the Piggly Wiggly spot down the street, opened this new, bigger supermarket with a huge parking lot (200 spaces) and a prominent sign in 1959. The Sewell chain merged with Mayfair in 1966, and Statewide Lighting took over the spot at 1331 South Virginia Street in 1973. *Author photos*

Clockwise from top left: The Vacation Motor Lodge (opened 1958), Thunderbird Motel (1958), and 777 Motel (1964) each offered a place to spend the night for travelers along old U.S. 395 in Reno. *Author photos*

South Virginia Street resorts: The Atlantis (with pillar, below) began as the Golden Road Motor Inn in 1972 and underwent three name changes, and expansion, before becoming the Atlantis in 1996. The Peppermill opened as a coffee shop and lounge in 1971, expanding substantially in 1986. *Author photos*

High Sierra Lanes at Virginia Street and Moana Lane, between Atlantis and the Peppermill, actually predates them both. It opened in late 1958 as Town & Country Bowl, an $800,000 bowling center with 24 lanes, three dining areas, two kitchens, and a shop. The center got its current name when a new owner took over in 1997. *Author photos*

Finding Reno

Location: 86 miles south of Susanville and 16 miles south of the California state line; about 30 miles north of Carson City

Route: U.S. 395/Interstate 580; U.S. 395 Business/Virginia Street in town. Sierra Street downtown was once designated as 395 Alternate, and Kietzke Lane was 395 Temporary during the construction of I-580.

Landrum's, top, at 1300 South Virgina Street opened in 1947 and went through a number of changes; it's seen here as Beefy's Burgers in 2022. At just 240 square feet, Landrum's utilized the smallest model of prefabricated diner produced by Valentine Manufacturing, which shipped them all over the country in the 1940s and '50s. You could order bacon and eggs and chili-cheese omelets at Landrum's (which later became the Chili Cheez Café). A planned Landrum's chain never materialized, although the Cup Café, above, (later Kimmie's) farther south on Virginia started as an attempt to reboot Landrum's. *Author photos*

It's oddly appropriate that Carpeteria, a carpet shop with an Aladdin-themed sign, is less than a mile up the road from Magic Carpet Golf, which offers 66 holes of mini-sized fun on three courses and an arcade at the south end of town.
Author photos

A frog prince, Easter Island head, and two-headed dragon are among the colorful obstacles at Magic Carpet Golf, which opened in 1974. The family-owned company also runs courses in South Lake Tahoe and Carnelian Bay, on the lake's north shore. From dinosaurs to a giant ant, all the sculptures were designed by Lee Koplin, who created other courses in places like Panama City Beach in Florida, and Tucson. *Author photos*

A fortune teller sign and the distinctive top-hatted motel sign are among the blasts from the past still visible just south of Reno. The Merry Wink has been there since 1942. The eye on the neon sign used to wink, but it no longer lights up. A series of Burma Shave-style signs promoting the motel nearby once read something like: "The man who drives - half asleep - is now buried - six feet deep." *Author photos*

STEAMBOAT SPRINGS

Eleven miles south of Reno, Nevada. Under new management. Hottest and highest mineralized waters in the world. Cures all diseases. Natural hot steam and bath tub baths. Trout stream and shade park on grounds. First class bar in connection. First class board. Rates $10 per week and up. Daily mail. Four trains daily. Round trip from Reno, 50c. Old fashioned chicken dinner on Sundays, 50c. Address.

MRS. M. L. PHENIX, Steamboat, Nevada

You can still take old 395 south of Reno into Washoe Valley, where it's signed as 395 Alternate, by simply continuing south on Virginia Street. One of the first places you'll come to is Steamboat Springs, one of many natural hot springs along the Sierra Highway that attracted tourists—including, in the early 1860s, a young reporter from Virginia City named Mark Twain. It once featured a 70-foot geyser, and a town grew up around the attraction that included a hotel built in 1860 and a railroad station in 1871. But an earthquake at the turn of the 20th century shifted the ground, stopped up the geyser, and affected the springs. In 2023, however, a health resort (above) still operates there. *Author photo, 1913 newspaper ad*

Washoe Valley

The north end of Washoe Valley, overlooking Little Washoe Lake. *Author photo*

On the highway, 1914

"According to County Commissioner George Kitzmeyer, the east side of Washoe Lake is the best route for autoists between this city and Reno. While considerable sand is encountered on the east side after passing Douglas Ranch, better time is made than by attempting the road on the west side, which is full of chuck holes and is about three miles the longer route."

— *Carson City Daily Appeal, August 14*

A year after that account was printed, a suggestion put forth in the *Reno Gazette* sparked a controversy that spanned nearly a decade and eventually shook the halls of state government.

SIERRA HIGHWAY

The original Lincoln Highway, as laid out in 1913, ran along the west side of the lake, following today's U.S. 395 Alternate and Franktown Road. But there were those who thought Nevada would be better off investing in a state highway on the east side of the lake, where the existing road seemed in better shape—apart from the sandy section Kitzmeyer had mentioned.

"Persons who are constantly using the Reno-Carson road are now using the road running on the east side of Washoe Lake, which is in much better condition than the west side," the *Gazette* reported in the summer of 1916.

By December 1919, the road was being graveled to eliminate the three-mile-long sandy section that had caused the most problems. And later that month, following a survey of the west-side route, State Highway Department chairman W.B. Alexander announced that Nevada had chosen the east side for its official concrete route.

The west-side road ran through the sleepy town of Washoe City, which had been the county seat in the 1860s before Reno took up the mantle. The east side was even more sparsely populated. (New Washoe City wouldn't be founded until a century later, as a planned community, in 1961.) While the west side was more scenic, east-side construction would be cheaper, and there were fewer railroad crossings and difficult grades than in the west.

And that, it appeared, was that.

But not so fast. Businessman Harry Riter led a group of several west-side farmers in filing a protest against the decision. Riter, the owner of a brewery in Reno, had purchased the historic Bowers Mansion on the west side of Washoe Valley in 1903 and converted it into a resort. He therefore had quite the vested interest in making it accessible to travelers.

Riter immediately appealed the decision to Governor Emmet D. Boyle, who was known to be sympathetic to the west-side option. (Riter reportedly reminded Boyle of a pre-election campaign promise to ensure the road ran along the west side.)

You can see what the proposed state highway on the eastern shore would have looked like on the following page.

SIERRA HIGHWAY

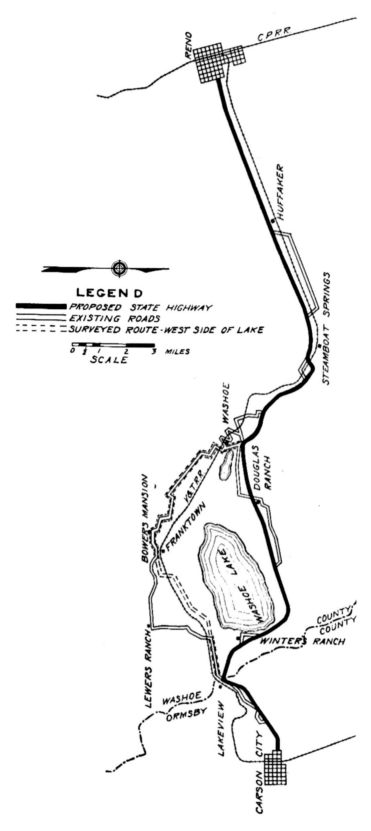

Bowers Mansion was built in 1863 by Lemuel "Sandy" Bowers and his wife, Eilley, who had made their fortune in Comstock mining. After Sandy Bowers' death, his widow kept herself afloat financially by renting out rooms and hosting gala parties there. She finally lost the mansion to foreclosure in 1876, and it sat abandoned before Henry Riter took possession of it. *Author photo*

Would have.

Sure enough, a week after the initial decision was made, Boyle cited numbers from state highway engineer C.C. Cottrell to contradict Alexander's claim that the eastern road could be built for less.

He added that the western route wasn't significantly longer, and it could be cleared of snow just as easily. The *Gazette* printed the full text of letters between the two men, with Boyle laying out nine reasons that the western route was to be preferred. Alexander, however, defended his decision, saying that both Cottrell and his predecessor as state engineer had recommended the eastern route, which was also favored by Washoe County commissioners.

Boyle's response? He removed Alexander from his position on the three-member state highway board of directors.

This, in turn, prompted another director, George K. Elder, to resign. That left just a single director (who had, not coincidentally, favored the west-side route) on the board, which no longer had a working majority.

Once the board was functional again, there was little doubt as to which side of the issue (and the lake) it would come down upon. The initial decision was reversed, and the nod went to the west side—where both U.S. 395 and Interstate 580 eventually ran. The second generation of the Lincoln Highway, however, switched from the west side to the east side of the lake, where an alternate route called Eastlake Boulevard now runs.

Franktown Road, a segment of the original west Washoe Valley road, still exists today as State Route 877. Founded in 1855, it was the site of a quartz mill that employed hundreds of workers and served as the hub of a farming community. The mill went into decline in 1869, and the town's name is about all that remains. A few miles to the south was Lakeview, at the pass between Carson City and Washoe Valley, where two hotels stood by 1863—one of which became a station on the Virginia and Truckee Railroad. *Author photos*

Above: Rancho Del Sierra, the house on Winters Ranch along U.S. 395 Alternate, was built by Theodore Winters in 1862 after he made a fortune off the Ophir Mine in the Comstock, three miles west of Washoe. The ranch once encompassed 6,000 acres, including a horse racing track, an orchard, and livestock. In the late 1800s, Winters was the largest landholder in Washoe Valley; his family continued to live in the home until 1953.

Below: Washoe Valley, looking east across Washoe Lake. *Author photos*

Prize Fight in Washoe Valley

Mark Twain, a contemporary of Bowers and Winters, once covered a boxing match in Washoe for the Territorial Enterprise newspaper of Virgina City. A crowd of 1,200 gathered to see Billy McGrath fight Tom Daly, and some in the crowd were less than pleased when Daly was declared the winner on a foul. An excerpt from Twain's account follows:

Harry Lazarus had been betting freely on McGrath, and was loud in his denunciation of the referee, and everybody who agreed with him in his decision. A Mexican by the name of Epitacis A. Maldanado, alias "Muchach," had been betting on Daly, and kept crying out that the blow was foul. Lazarus called him a liar, and pistols were immediately drawn.

As soon as Lazarus and "Much" commenced firing, two or three other parties joined in (so we are told), but we were unable to learn their names... Two horses were shot in the melee, and the only wonder is that more men were not struck by the random pistol balls that flew singing through the air in every direction...

Returning to the ring we found it almost deserted, the wounded men, "Muchach" and Lazarus, having been carried to the saloon near the gate of the enclosure. Thither we repaired and found "Muchach" lying on a table, stripped to the waist, with a ball hole in his right breast, close to the nipple, another near the pit of his stomach, and we were told that another ball had entered his side and another struck one of his arms.

On another table, stripped likewise to the waist, lay Harry Lazarus, who had escaped without any apparent serious injuries... His hand was struck while he was in the act of leveling his pistol, and it is thought, the ball which entered his breast was the same that shattered his fingers. At the time we left Washoe, about four o'clock in the afternoon, "Muchach" was still alive, but was not expected to survive long.

Top: The former Washoe City Jail is now a Garden Center. It's the only building still intact from the days when the town served as the seat of Washoe County.

Above: The south end of Washoe Valley, overlooking Washoe Lake with Eastlake Boulevard at left. *Author photos*

The Chocolate Nugget Candy Factory, with its giant prospector has been open since 1983 just south of the 395 Alt. offramp in Washoe City. *Author photos*

Driving north into Reno on I-580/U.S. 395 in December 2022 was a challenge as the region dealt with an unusually snowy winter, but it still wasn't as bad as it had been 70 years earlier. The blizzard of January 1952 buried Donner Summit under 65 feet of snow and trapped 226 passengers on a snowbound luxury train over the Sierra for three days before rescuers arrived. *Author photo*

On the highway, 1952

"U.S. 395 south was closed by [snow] drifts between Reno and Carson City... In Washoe Valley, snowplows weren't even working. 'It'd be useless as well as dangerous to our men and equipment,' a spokesman said. To the north, the same route was closed on the north city limits of Reno. Travel to Susanville was impossible last night."

— *Nevada State Journal, January 22*

More scenes along I-580/U.S. 395 in December 2022 show skeletal trees and a snow-blotched mileage sign beside the highway. *Author photos*

Snow isn't the only form of natural disaster that troubles Washoe Valley. Landslides are another threat, as made plain by the name of a mountain on the west side of the Valley: Slide Mountain. Mark Twain even wrote about it in his book *Roughing It*.

"The mountains are very high and steep about Carson, Eagle and Washoe Valleys—very high and very steep, and so when the snow gets to melting off fast in the Spring and the warm surface-earth begins to moisten and soften, the disastrous land-slides commence. The reader cannot know what a land-slide is, unless he has lived in that country and seen the whole side of a mountain taken off some fine morning and deposited down in the valley, leaving a vast, treeless, unsightly scar upon the mountain's front to keep the circumstance fresh in his memory all the years that he may go on living within seventy miles of that place."

Twain went on to tell the story of "The Great Landslide Case."

The case in question was a lawsuit resulting from a particular Washoe landslide. The catastrophe deposited a house owned by a rancher named Morgan directly on top of a home belonging to his neighbor, Dick Hyde. The neighbor sued, enlisting the help of the U.S. Attorney, General Buncombe.

Hyde was livid, saying Morgan had refused to vacate the site and demanded justice. Buncombe dutifully took the case, which ended up in the courtroom of none other than Isaac Roop, the former territorial governor who was involved in the Susanville fracas dubbed Roop's war.

This dispute turned out to be much less serious. In fact, it was all just a big practical joke being played on the lawyer, Buncombe. Roop, who was in on the joke, ruled against him, declaring, "I warn you that this thing which has happened is a thing with which the sacrilegious hands and brains and tongues of men must not meddle. Gentlemen, it is the verdict of this court that the plaintiff, Richard Hyde, has been deprived of his ranch by the visitation of God! And from this decision there is no appeal."

Buncombe, whom Twain described as "an impatient and irascible man," exited the courtroom, indignant, declaring Roop to be "a miraculous fool, an inspired idiot."

He nevertheless implored the judge to go for a walk, so he might persuade him to change his mind. After Buncombe had spent an hour and a half arguing, Roop finally seemed to come around. He said it now occurred to him that the ranch underneath Morgan's relocated ranch still belonged to Hyde—who therefore had every right to dig it out!

The chagrined lawyer didn't even wait to hear the end of Roop's reasoning, but left in a huff, humiliated.

Eighty years later, in 1952, the Reno Chamber of Commerce suggested changing the mountain's name to Mount Reno, so visitors could locate it on the map more easily—especially in light of plans for an all-year resort in the area called Reno Bowl. (Never mind that it's also clearly visible from Carson City.) Plus, they said, Slide Mountain had a negative connotation.

But opponents were having nothing of it, pointing to its historical use, on maps since as early as 1862, as well as the connection to Twain. In the end, the proposal died, and the Slide Mountain name endured.

On the highway, 1983

"It should be no surprise that a landslide on Slide Mountain apparently triggered the wall of mud and debris that washed out roads and homes Monday near Bowers Mansion Park. About 120 years ago, a huge landslide, estimated to be eight times larger than Mondays, crashed down the mountain, giving it the name Slide Mountain... H.B. "Doc" Smith, a U.S. Forest Service supervisor... estimated that about 40 acres of the mountain slid down the slope... The mud juggernaut washed out old Highway 395, between Davis Creek Park and Bowers Mansion Park. It flowed through a meadow and, after running almost parallel to new Highway 395, dumped into Washoe Lake."

— *Phil Barber and Richard Moreno,*
Reno Gazette-Journal, May 31

The barren slope of Slide Mountain shows how it got its name. *Author photo*

Above: Wild horses, such as these seen near Steamboat Springs, are a common sight along 395 south of Reno, where they're often seen grazing beside Washoe Lake.

Right: Signs like this one on Eastlake Boulevard warn drivers to be on the lookout. *Author photos*

Overhead signs point the way south to Minden or north to Reno via Interstate 580/U.S. 395, and straight ahead to downtown Carson City. *Author photo*

County: Carson City *(state capital; Ormsby County seat until 1969)*

Elevation: 4,682

Established: 1858

Incorporated: 1875

> **1920** — Population: 1,685
>
> **2020** — Population: 58,639

Key buildings on 395:

> St. Charles Hotel (1862)
>
> Carson City Mint/Nevada State Museum (1863)
>
> Nevada State Capitol (1871)
>
> Bank Saloon (1899)
>
> Carson City Post Office/Laxalt Building (1891)
>
> Carson City Nugget (1954)

Looking north on Carson Street near the north end of the capital. Slide Mountain can be seen at far left. *Author photo*

Coming down from Lakeview to the north, you enter Carson City almost immediately. Today, you have a choice: You can bypass downtown and continue on Interstate 580 (which is also modern 395), or you can exit on Carson Street and travel through the state capital on the old highway, now known as Business 395.

But not so long ago, you wouldn't have had that option. The I-580 bypass wasn't complete until 2012, just six years after the northern section of the freeway opened. Before that, you had to drive through the heart of Carson City to continue south.

A lot has changed in Carson City. For about a century, it was the seat of Ormsby County. But in 1969, services of the city and county were consolidated, and Ormsby County was wiped off the map. Thenceforth, Carson City was its own county, a unique situation in Nevada similar to San Francisco's status in California.

These days, Carson Street is just two lanes as it passes through the heart of downtown, widening to four lanes north of William Street, the northern junction of U.S. 50, and again south of the Carson Mall at a recent innovation: a traffic circle where it joins Stewart Street.

On the highway, 2020

"The intersection of Carson and Stewart streets was, for decades, just a basic three-way stoplight. Now it is being reshaped into a roundabout, serving as an entrance to downtown Carson City."

— *Scott Schrantz, Around Carson, October 20*

U.S. 50 and 395 run together through downtown for just over 4 miles before the former branches off west again toward South Lake Tahoe through Clear Creek Canyon. The second alignment of the Lincoln Highway left modern Carson Street near here, too, although the original version of that highway ascended the Sierra Nevada via Kings Canyon Road—today nothing more than a rocky dirt road west of town.

Carson City is one of several places in Nevada named in honor of the explorer, Christopher "Kit" Carson. (The Carson River and the Carson Valley, just to the south, are others.) Carson City has designated a 2.5-mile route through its historic district as the Kit Carson Trail, which passes nearly 50 historical landmarks and is marked by sidewalk emblems such as the one pictured at left, on Carson Street. All of them postdate Carson's brief time in the area: He made expeditions to Nevada in 1844 and again in 1853, both times en route to California.

Other famous figures were far more instrumental in the history of Carson City. Among them was Abraham Curry, who not only founded the city but was an original partner in the famous Gould & Curry Mine discovered at Virginia City in 1859. (Curry sold his share of the mine before he could make the kind of fortune others would find in the Comstock, and his partner, Alva Gould, infamously sold his share for peanuts to George Hearst, who used it to make a fortune that would help his son build a newspaper empire and a California castle.)

Even more famous was Samuel Clemens, who lived with his brother Orion in Carson City for a time while working for the *Virginia City Territorial Enterprise* in the early 1860s. Clemens, aka Mark Twain, would only live in Nevada for about three years, but it was there that he made the connections that would pave the way for his future success as a writer and orator.

Carson City has been the state capital ever since Nevada's admission to the Union in 1864. Never the state's largest city—as of 2020 it ranked No. 6—it was for many years the smallest state capital in the nation, having grown by just 40 persons from its 1870 population of 3,042 eight decades later.

On the highway, 1956

"A tourist motoring south from Reno on U.S. 395 comes to this pleasant little town after a drive of about thirty miles. Carson City is the smallest state capital of any in the forty-eight states."

— Ward Allan Howe,
New York Times, December 30

Its population, however, tripled in size from barely 5,000 to more than 15,000 in 1970, following its consolidation with Ormsby County, and it more than doubled again before the decade was out. It's been the home of such notables as Nevada governor and U.S. Senator Paul Laxalt, a onetime Republican presidential hopeful; George Washington Gale Ferris Jr., inventor of the Ferris Wheel; and famed stagecoach driver Hank Monk, who made his base of operations the St. Charles Hotel on Carson Street downtown.

The St. Charles Hotel on Carson Street was built way back in 1862 and housed the offices of the Pioneer Stage Company. It changed its name to the Briggs in 1890, and later became the Golden West, the Travelers, and, in 1953, the Pony Express Hotel before reverting to its original name. In the background at left and below is the Ormsby House hotel and casino, built by Paul Laxalt in 1972. It became the city's tallest and, for the past two decades, most conspicuously vacant building after the business went belly-up. *Author photos*

Travelers on a budget could stay at one of the many motels that once lined Carson Street at the north and south ends of the city. In the 21st century, only a few, such as the Frontier Motel—with its signature neon cowboy—and Carson City Inn remained. The Frontier dated back more than 80 years, having started out as Dorothy's Auto Court. Others with names like the Carson Motor Lodge/Whistle Stop Inn, Nevada Auto Court, Ranch-Otel, Taylor Court, and DeLuxe are now gone. *Author photos*

Left: A Lincoln Highway marker in front of the Carson City Mint on Carson Street. Nearly 3 million Morgan silver dollars were minted there. The building functioned as an assay office until 1933 and now houses part of the Nevada State Museum. *Author photo*

Above: The Carson City Mint once sat in an open field. It was established in 1863 to mint coins in response to the Comstock silver strike, but ground wasn't broken until 1866, and the building—constructed under the supervision of city founder Abraham Curry—finally opened in 1870. On February 11 of that year, the mint began producing "Seated Silver Dollars" with the CC mint mark and, it produced 57 types of coins before closing for good in 1893. The large chimney atop the building was once even taller than shown here. *Library of Congress*

Above: The Nevada State Capitol on U.S. 395 was designed by San Francisco architect Joseph Gosling and completed in 1871. The builder, Peter Cavanaugh & Son of Carson City, used locally quarried sandstone for the building but grossly underestimated its cost: Its bid of $84,000 barely covered half the final price tag, and that didn't count the furnishings, which were $20,000 more. *Author photos*

Right: The Nevada State Legislative building on 395 was completed in 1971.

Above: The Bank Saloon, aka Jack's Bar, was built on the northwest corner of Carson Street and 5th Street in 1899. When it was placed on the National Register of Historic Places in 1980, it was the oldest continuously operating drinking establishment in Carson City, even weathering Prohibition. *Author photo*

Left: 1967 map from newspaper ad.

Finding Carson City

Location: 30 miles south of Reno; 19 miles north of Minden

Route: Interstate 580 bypass; Carson Street / Business 395

Above: The Dutch Mill food stand, founded in 1935, sported a big windmill at the indersection of U.S. 50 and 395, serving up Chism Ice Cream, Coca-Cola, burgers, and more. *Nevada Armored Transport*

Left: The stand had evolved into a full restaurant by the 1950s, and became Heidi's in 1986. *Author photo*

Top: The Carson Nugget, with an entrance modeled after the Golden Nugget in Las Vegas, opened in 1954, before the much larger Nugget in Sparks. It's the oldest casino in the city. *Author photo*

Above: Grand opening ad, featuring the casino's mascot, Last Chance Joe, and its signature Awful-AWFUL SANDWICH (author photo, left).

Top: Cactus Jack's, across 395, was originally known as the Senator Club until the name was changed in 1971. *Author photo*

Above: This building (here c. the 1940s and also at above left) underwent a name change too. Built as the U.S. Post Office and Courthouse in 1891, it stopped being used as a post office in 1970 and was deeded to the state a year later. It was renamed the Paul Laxalt State Building in 1999.

Left: Unlike Route 66, not many businesses use 395 as part of their name. An exception is Red's Old 395 Grill on Carson Street.

Below: A locomotive at the Nevada Railroad Museum on Carson Street, which opened in 1980, and Virginia & Truckee Railroad Depot on old 395. *Author photos*

DETOUR ▶ Genoa

If you're looking for Genoa while cruising down 395, this sign shows where to turn. It's about four miles west of the highway on Genoa Lane. If you plan to visit, however, you should expect a lot of traffic one weekend in September. The annual Candy Dance, a celebration that began in 1919 as a fund-raiser to install streetlights, draws tens of thousands of people each year, with law enforcement out directing traffic on the highway. The event's name comes from a suggestion that a dance be held, and that candy be passed out during the event to boost attendance. The dance was a success and turned into an annual tradition—because even after the streetlights were purchased, money still had to be raised for the electric bill to keep them on. *Author photo*

Finding Genoa

Location: About 15 miles south of Carson City; about 7 miles northwest of Minden

Route: State Route 206 (Jack's Valley Road-Foothill Road).

Above: Main Street through Genoa in 1940, with the Genoa Bar & Saloon at left. It had already been there nearly a century by that point, having opened in 1853. *Arthur Rothstein, Library of Congress*

Right: The Genoa Bar & Saloon in 2023. Among those said to have sidled up to the bar there are Mark Twain, Teddy Roosevelt, and John Wayne. *Author photo*

SIERRA HIGHWAY

Genoa's claim to be the oldest permanent (non-native) settlement in Nevada dates back to the Mormon Station trading post and stockade, established on the Carson Route of the California Trail in 1851. Mormon settlers in the area left six years later and returned to Utah when Brigham Young called them back to defend Salt Lake City against U.S. troops. *Author photos*

This replica of the station is at the center of town, and the surrounding park hosts community events in addition to serving as a reminder of Genoa's place in history.

Top: The original Mormon Station, which burned in 1910, was a Pony Express stop in 1860 and '61. *Wikipedia*

Above: The replica, seen here In 1958, was built in 1947. *National Park Service*

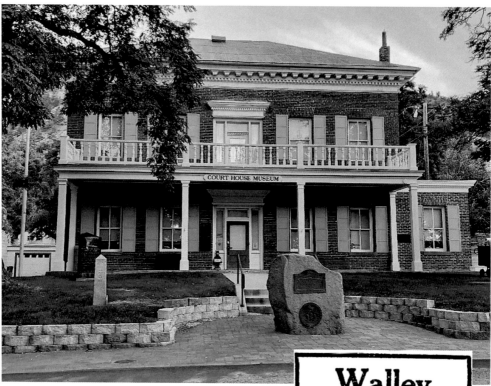

Above: Genoa was the seat of Douglas County until 1916 (when the county seat moved to Minden in recognition of the latter community's place on the Virginia & Truckee rail line), with government business being conducted in this courthouse built in 1865. It later became the Genoa School and currently serves as a museum. The county is named for Stephen A. Douglas, Abraham Lincoln's opponent in the famous Lincoln-Douglas debates of 1858. *Author photos*

Right: A 1911 ad for Walley's Hot Springs, which opened in 1862 just south of Genoa. Mark Twain is said to have visited the springs, as he did Steamboat Springs and Curry's Warm Springs in Carson City.

The two buildings at right in the top photo, taken by Arthur Rothstein
in 1940, are seen in a 2023 photo by the author at bottom on Jack's
Valley Road, which is Main Street through Genoa.

END
DETOUR

Minden Park, a block off the highway on Esmeralda Avenue (the town's main street), dates back to the founding of Minden in 1906. The original bandstand was added in 1914, and the one seen here dates to 1984. *Author photo*

Minden

County: Douglas *(county seat)*

Elevation: 4,725

Established: 1906

Unincorporated

> **1920** — Population: 440
>
> **2020** — Population: 3,442

Key buildings on 395:

> Minden Flour Milling Co. (1908)
>
> The Heidelberg/Francisco's (1910)
>
> C.O.D. Garage (1911)
>
> Carson Valley Inn (1984)

The Minden Flour Milling Co. was the first new business in the town of Minden. Founded in 1906, it completed its mill in 1908 with 45-foot-tall flour silos capable of holding up to 65,000 bushels of grain. By the 1920s, the plant was churning out 100 barrels of flour a day, along with chicken and cattle feed. It continued to operate until 1960 and remains one of the most visible structures along U.S. 395.

Author photos

Finding Minden

Location: About 15 miles south of Carson City; adjacent to Gardnerville

Route: U.S. Highway 395

Left: The former C.O.D. Garage in Minden, just off the highway, is now a casino. Built in 1911, it sold a variety of makes and models over the years, including Hupmobiles, Fords, and Chevys. *Author photos*

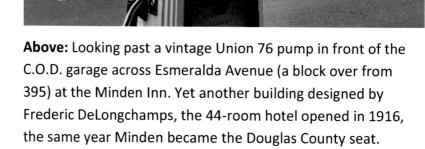

Above: Looking past a vintage Union 76 pump in front of the C.O.D. garage across Esmeralda Avenue (a block over from 395) at the Minden Inn. Yet another building designed by Frederic DeLongchamps, the 44-room hotel opened in 1916, the same year Minden became the Douglas County seat.

Above: Carson Valley Inn hotel and casino opened in 1984 and was operated for a quarter-century by Patrick and Jeane Mulreany. It was sold in 2009 to the operators of Bodine's Casino in Carson City and the Eldorado and Silver Legacy in Reno.

Below: The Central Valley Improvement Club's CVIC Hall dates back to 1912 and has hosted everything from basketball games to funerals over the years. *Author photos*

Top: Francisco's Mexican Restaurant sits on a diagonal corner entrance from 395 into downtown. The building has been there since 1910, when it opened as the Heidelberg Bar. It housed a grocery store and soda fountain during Prohibition, then in 1941 became a bar again—the Pony Express, which remained in business for six decades before Francisco's took over.

Above: Farmer's Bank of Carson Valley was founded in this building in 1909. When the bank moved into larger digs 10 years later, the post office moved in and operated there until 1974. *Author photos*

The second Farmer's Bank of Carson Valley succeeded the smaller building on the previous page and operated until 1968, weathering the Depression.
Author photo

Getting there, 1918

Directions from Carson City south to Minden, according to the 1918 Automobile Blue Book, with miles between each entry:

0.0 mile: South Carson & West King Sts., state capitol on left. Go south on South Carson Street.

1.0 mile: Fork; bear left onto gravel road across prairie.

1.9 miles: Fork; bear right.

1.8 miles: Fork; bear right with travel.

2.7 miles: Fork, sign in center; bear left with poles.

7.7 miles: Caution—left-hand road; turn left, leaving poles.

0.7 mile: 4-corners, school on right; turn right 1 short block and left at 4-corners just beyond.

0.3 mile: Minden, ahead on Main St.

0.2 mile: End of street, lumber yard on left; turn left, onto Main St.

Looking north on U.S. 395 (highway sign at left) as it curves into Gardnerville. The town traces its roots to 1879, when Lawrence Gilman purchased the Kent House just south of Genoa, which was reputed to be haunted by a ghost who robbed stagecoaches. Gilman moved the house to land he acquired from John Gardner and turned it into the Gardnerville Hotel. *Author photo*

Gardnerville

County: Douglas

Elevation: 4,751

Established: 1879

Unincorporated

>   **1930** — Population: 658

>   **2020** — Population: 6,211

Key buildings on 395:

>   Arendt Jensen Merchandise (1896)

>   French Bar (1914)

>   Douglas County High School (1915)

>   Sharkey's Casino (1946)

Sharkey's in Gardnerville opened in 1946 as the Golden Bubble Casino on U.S. 395. At the time, Gardnerville had somewhere between 600 and 1,000 residents, between 10 and 20 percent of its current population. There'd been a corner saloon there as far back as the 1890s, when the surrounding business district included a blacksmith shop, drugstore, and mortuary. Milos "Sharkey" Begovich later purchased the Golden Bubble and changed the name to Sharkey's Nugget (later just Sharkey's). He made it famous for its inch-thick prime rib, Christmas dinners, appearances by country stars like Waylon Jennings and Willie Nelson, and collection of boxing memorabilia. He even staged prize fights at the local baseball field. Sharkey sold the place in 2001, shortly before his death, but it still bears his name. *Author photos*

Finding Gardnerville

Location: Just south of and adjacent to Minden (the two are often named together as Minden-Gardnerville), and about 23 miles northwest of the Nevada state line
Route: U.S. Highway 395

Top: The speed limit is 25 mph through Minden and Gardnerville on 395.

Above: Douglas County High School, designed by Frederic DeLongchamps, opened in 1915 on future U.S. 395. It later became a middle school and now serves as the Carson Valley Museum & Cultural Center. The new high school, called simply Douglas High, is on State Route 88 in Minden. *Author photos*

The Overland Restaurant and Pub opened in 1902 as a meat market, hotel, restaurant, and pub catering to Basque sheepherders in Carson Valley. *Author photos*

The J.T. Basque Bar and Dining Room, above, and the French Bar, at left, both on U.S. 395, are evidence of the heavy Basque influence in Gardnerville. The J.T. opened in 1955, and the French dates back to 1914. Teams from across the state competed in the traditional handball game called pilota at the French.

The large brick Masonic Hall
dominates the southern end
of downtown on U.S. 395.
Arendt Jensen built the structure
with the arched front on the far side of the street (inset) as a mercantile in
1896 and sold the lot next door to the Masons in 1919. *Author photos*

On the highway, 1951

"Prison convict Candelario R. Caballero flagged the wrong
car this morning. The 21-year-old Mexican broke away
from gang work near the prison farm Wednesday
afternoon and was nabbed after an intensive search at 6
a.m. today just off U.S. 395 near Minden. He was caught
as he attempted to flag a ride from a passing motorist.
Unfortunately for him, that driver was A.E. Bernard,
warden of the state prison, who with guard Herman
Smoot was out looking for him. Bernard obliged by
stopping the car, took Caballero aboard and transferred
him back to state prison where he was immediately put
in solitary confinement."

— *Reno Evening Gazette, May 10*

Topaz Lake

Topaz Lake marks the last stop in Nevada heading south on 395 before entering California on the Eastern Sierra Scenic Byway portion of the highway. A 1952 ad seeking a lessee at the lodge described it as "the first chance to dine, drink and gamble on entering Nevada." The lodge was a "brand new ultra-modern two-story brick and redwood" lodge. *Author photos*

Following page: A 1957 ad for the lodge.

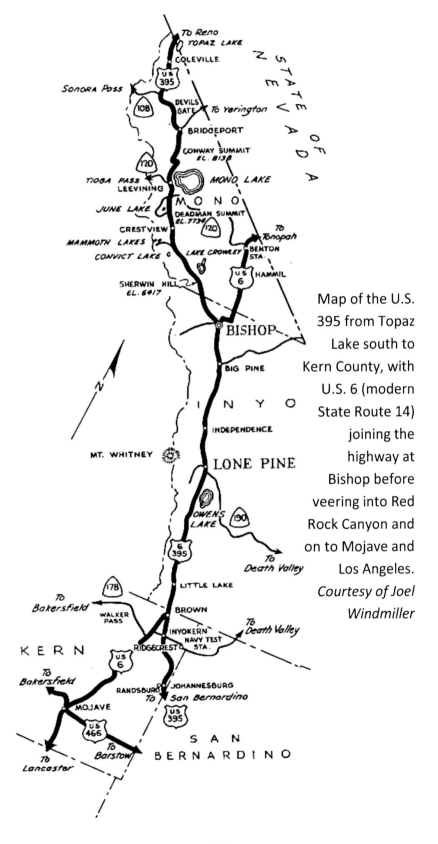

Map of the U.S. 395 from Topaz Lake south to Kern County, with U.S. 6 (modern State Route 14) joining the highway at Bishop before veering into Red Rock Canyon and on to Mojave and Los Angeles. *Courtesy of Joel Windmiller*

A 1954 monument marking Monitor Pass, one of three passes from 395 across the Sierra, is seen at left. Above, the view from just east of the pass, looking down over a valley a few miles west of 395. The road comes out just north of Coleville. *Author photo, above; Sharon Marie Provost, left*

U.S. 395 meets California State Route 108 at Sonora Junction, seen here closed for the winter in 2022. *Author photo*

Mono County
Topaz Lake to Bishop   134 miles

When you mention the Sierra Highway, many people will envision this stretch of road. It is, after all, the section most synonymous with the High Sierra.

Instead of running along the base of the mountains as it does in Nevada and Inyo County, U.S. 395 in Mono County carves a path through and over the top of them. The county is home to California's three highest mountain passes: Monitor, Sonora, and Tioga—with 395 serving as the gateway to each one of them.

State Route 89, traveling west from the south end of Topaz Lake, takes you across Monitor Pass at an elevation of 8,314 feet en route to

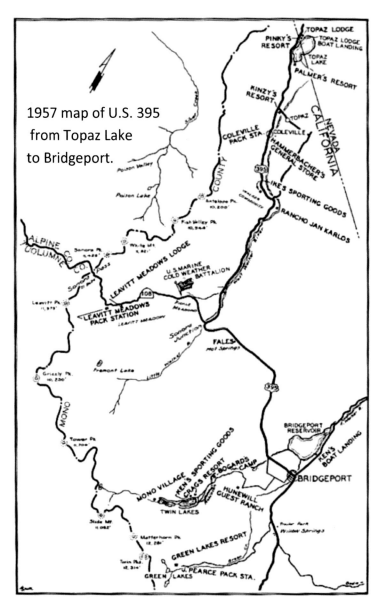

1957 map of U.S. 395 from Topaz Lake to Bridgeport.

Markleeville, a stop on the original Pasear Tour. Less than 30 miles to the south is Sonora Junction, where State Route 108 branches off westward and heads even higher into the Sierra, reaching 9,624 feet at Sonora Pass on its way to the San Joaquin Valley. But the highest of them all is Tioga Pass (9,945 feet), accessed via State Route 120 at Lee Vining, which takes

motorists to Yosemite Valley—if the pass is open. During winter, it typically isn't.

U.S. 395 itself doesn't get quite that high, but elevations of 7,000 feet or more are common in Mono County. Devil's Gate Pass southeast of Bridgeport will take you up to 7,519 feet; Conway Summit, north of the descent toward Mono Lake, rises to 8,143 feet; and Deadman

Summit north of Mammoth Lakes is nearly as high at 8,047 feet.

Hot springs and lakes are most prevalent along this section of road, the most impressive of the latter being Mono Lake, a remnant of a much larger lake known as Lake Russell that dates to the Pleistocene Era (i.e., the Ice Age that ended nearly 12,000 years ago). The two islands in the middle of the lake, called Negit and Paoha, were formed by volcanic activity in the area that occurred as recently as 300 years ago.

U.S. 395 winds down from Conway Summit toward Mono Lake.
Author photo

Tufa formations along the south shore of Mono Lake in 2023. *Author photo*

A nearly circular salt lake, Mono is home to brine shrimp, shorebirds such as killdeer and sandpipers that feed on them, and the famous tufa formations: calcium carbonate towers formed as freshwater springs percolate up through sediments on the lake's bottom and its saltwater. They're most prominent on the lake's south shore, and more are still forming today.

SIERRA HIGHWAY

As impressive as Mono Lake is, it's far from the only natural beauty you'll encounter on this part of the road. Before you get there, if you're traveling south, you'll spend several miles driving alongside the Walker River north of Bridgeport. This watercourse starts off in the Bridgeport Valley and flows north along 395 for about 30 miles before veering east in Nevada, eventually emptying into Walker Lake along U.S. Highway 95.

A car navigates the Sierra Highway alongside the Walker River during the Pasear Tour in 1912.
McCurry Foto

SIERRA HIGHWAY

In documenting the Pasear Tour, the McCurry Foto Company of Sacramento took several pictures along the Walker River, an area no less picturesque today as it was then.

Driving along the Walker River, seen at center, in 2023. *Author photo*

The highway and the Walker River In 2023 (author photo), and 1912 (McCurry Foto, inset).

SIERRA HIGHWAY

South of Mono Lake, you'll come upon more scenic beauty in the form of pine trees, snow-capped mountains, and shimmering lakes. The Mammoth Lakes area offers a host of recreational opportunities, from boating in the summertime to skiing at Mammoth Mountain in the winter. But it's far from the only attraction along this scenic stretch of highway.

Convict Lake offers breathtaking beauty along with trout fishing and hiking beyond Mammoth Lakes heading south, just a couple of miles southwest of 395. The lake's name stems from an incident in 1871, when a posse cornered a gang of escaped convicts from the State Prison in Carson City at the lake, killing two of them and recapturing most of the rest. *Author photos*

Coleville

Hammerbacher's Market and an old gas station, both closed, sit along U.S. 395 in Coleville, home to 419 people in 2020. The market housed a post office until 1957, when it moved to its own building.
Author photos

Finding Coleville

Location: About 10 miles south of the Nevada state line and 4 miles north of Walker

Route: U.S. 395

Walker

Above: Walker Burger opened in 1982 on 395 in Walker, south of Coleville. It became a destination for travelers hankerin' for a burger, sandwich, shake, or "other good stuff" on the menu like chicken salad, fish and slaw, or the "Danger Dog" with onions, bacon bits, and grilled jalapenos.

Below: The Toiyabe Motel opened in the late 1950s. *Author photos*

Getting there, 1918

Directions for navigating El Camino Sierra south from Gardnerville, 0.6 mile south of Minden, to Coleville, California, according to the 1918 Automobile Blue Book, with miles between each entry:

0.0 mile: Straight thru on Main St., follow phone line.

3.3 miles: Right-hand road, sign on right; turn right with poles. Avoid right-hand road (3 miles ahead), keeping ahead upgrade just beyond farm house.

11.4 miles: Fork; bear left. Pass mountain house on right, formerly Holbrook P.O., Nev.

4.0 miles: Fork; sign in center; bear right.

4.0 miles: Pass alkali lake on left.

9.1 miles: Pass cemetery on left.

0.9 mile: Coleville, Cal. Straight thru.

The Andruss Motel was born in 1960, when Ray and Margaret Andruss bought a four-room ranch-style building called Hickson's Fish Camp and expanded it, putting up the sign above. Today, it has "the only pool in Walker as long as you are willing to jump in," along with two horseshoe pits, and two gas and a pair of charcoal barbecues. Mono County's website describes it as "a classic American motor court for Eastern Sierra vacationers." *Author photo*

Finding Walker

Location: About 4 miles south of Coleville and 30 miles northwest of Bridgeport
Route: U.S. 395

Top: The Sierra Retreat Motel, built in 1973, catches motorists' attention with its distinctive canopied water wheel out front.

Above: The West Walker Motel dates back to 1945. *Author photos*

The Bridgeport Inn, with its big "Motor Motel" sign, reportedly played host to Mark Twain during a visit to Mono County (and has a Mark Twain Room to mark the occasion). Legend has it that a ghost dubbed the White Lady still lives there, having haunted Room 16 since the inn was known as Leavitt House in 1884. *Author photo*

Bridgeport

County: Mono *(county seat)*

Elevation: 6,463

Established: 1864

Unincorporated

     2020 — Population: 553

Key buildings on 395:

     Bridgeport Inn (1877)

     Mono County Courthouse (1880)

     Ken's Sporting Goods-Former Court House Corner Saloon (1883)

     Silver Maple Inn (1930s)

The 1880 courthouse in Bridgeport is actually Mono County's third courthouse. The first, a two-story brick building in the mining town of Aurora, had to be replaced because a survey found it was actually in Nevada, not California. County records were moved to Bodie and then to a second makeshift courthouse in Bridgeport, located in the former American Hotel (marker above). It was too small, though, so this courthouse was constructed. *Author photos*

Is the Silver Maple Motel haunted? There's no telling, but it could be. The motel, which stands next to the courthouse, just across School Street on 395, was built in the 1930s on or near the spot occupied by Bridgeport's original graveyard. The graves there were supposedly moved to a new cemetery. But a geophysical study revealed that only about 20 percent of the bodies were actually relocated. *Author photos*

A horse statue does a balancing act outside the Redwood Motel, a 1949-era inn near the northern entrance to Bridgeport. *Author photos*

Finding Bridgeport

Location: 45 miles southeast of the Topaz Lake and the Nevada state line; 25 miles north of Lee Vining

Route: U.S. 395/Main Street

Left: Ken's Sporting Goods, the former old Court House Corner Saloon, built in 1883 next to the courthouse.

Below: Other historic buildings line the north side of 395.
Author photos

Above: Jolly Kone has been in Bridgeport since 1964, serving up Frito pies, chili cheese dogs, shakes, and calamari fries. It stands along 395 on the site where one of the town founders, Amasa Bryant, opened a store in 1863.

Below: Virginia Creek Settlement five miles south of Bridgeport was opened as a restaurant in 1927 , with a five-unit motel added in 1954. *Author photos*

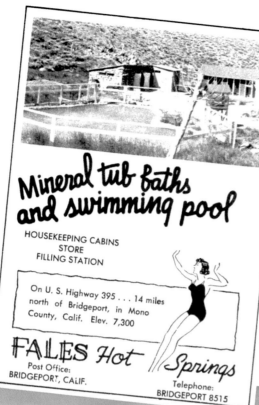

Left: Hot springs can be found on either side of Bridgeport, with Fales Hot Springs north of town, featured in this 1957 fishing and vacation guide ad. Samuel Fales developed a resort there in 1877, and it became a stage stop in 1908, but today it is on private land and inaccessible to the public.

Below: Travertine Hot Springs south of town, a tourist spot seen in 2022, once belonged to the Paiute Tribe and was thought to have been created by Isha, one of creation's overseers. *Author photo*

Bodie is one of the most complete ghost towns you're likely to find. It's also a state park. The mining town sprouted up just west of the Nevada state line in 1859 after William S. Bodey discovered gold near what became

Bodie Bluff and grew to a population of 10,000 by 1880. Mark Twain described Bodie as "the breakup of one winter and the beginning of the next." Miners had to endure brutal winters at 8,369 feet that could leave the entire town under 20 feet of snow, but they had 65 saloons to warm themselves with whiskey. Were those winters worth enduring? Thirty companies made $100 million in Bodie before the boom died. The site was designated a state historic park in 1962 and more than 100 buildings, such as the Dechambeau Hotel and Odd Fellows Lodge, seen at top, and the Miners' Union Hall, above, still stood. The hotel later became the Bodie Café, one of the last businesses to close. *Library of Congress*

Scenes from Bodie at the height of the boom in 1875. *California State University, Chico, Meriam Library Special Collections photos*

Above: Bodie around 1890. **Below:** of the bank building in 1926. *Historic American Buildings Survey, Library of Congress*

Finding Bodie

Location: 20 miles southeast of Bridgeport and 14 miles east of the highway; 32 miles northeast of Lee Vining

Route: State Route 270 east from 395 (dirt and gravel, 2-wheel-drive OK)

This U.S. Land Office was established in 1879 to deal with applications to purchase government land and moved to this building in 1885. A year later, with the town in decline, the office moved to Independence. The building, seen here in 1933, was later used as the office for the Power Company, the Bodie Store, and last of all the Wheaton and Hollis Hotel. Look through the windows to see this wood stove, which is still inside today, 80 years after this photo was taken.
Historic American Buildings Survey, Library of Congress

The Bodie Hotel building was moved to its present location on Highway 395 in Bridgeport in 1920. It's not the original hotel by that name, which burned to the ground in 1888. Oddly, a sign advertising "meals at all hours" at the Bodie Hotel is displayed inside the former Wheaton and Hollis Hotel at the Bodie State Park today. *Author photo*

In Bodie, 1888

"The Bodie Hotel, a large two-story-and-a-half frame building, was burned to the ground this morning… The halls were so filled with smoke that those in the upper story were compelled to jump out the windows to the balcony and then slide down the balcony posts. Few of the guests saved anything, not even their clothing. At one time the town was threatened with destruction. A miner by the name of Ed McCarthy, from Candelaria, was burned to death. The building was owned by O.H. Mill. Loss $10,000. Several people were hurt."

— Oakland Tribune, April 14

The 1879 Bon Ton Lodging House was converted into the new Bodie Schoolhouse, seen here in 1934. The first school burned to the ground after a boy who'd been sent home for getting in trouble started a fire in dry brush behind the structure. *Historic American Buildings Survey, Library of Congress*

Above: The road through Bodie facing west, with the schoolhouse at foreground right. The road continued eastward to Aurora, Nevada, where Mark Twain nearly struck it rich as a prospector in the early 1860s. *University of Southern California Libraries and California Historical Society*

Below: The Bodie Jail in 1925. *Historic American Buildings Survey, Library of Congress*

Top: The Catholic Church building in Bodie, right, no longer stands, having burned down a few years after it was dedicated in 1882. *University of Southern California Libraries and California Historical Society*

Above: The Methodist Church was built around the same time. They were the first two churches in Bodie. Before that, both congregations met in the Odd Fellows Hall. *Historic American Buildings Survey, Library of Congress*

Top: The Bodie Mill. *Historic American Buildings Survey, Library of Congress*

Above: Bodie as it appeared around 1930. *University of Southern California Libraries and California Historical Society*

Above: The Boone Store at Main and Green Streets, seen here in 1932, was owned by Harvey Boone—a direct descendant of Daniel Boone. Built in 1879, it survived a fire five years later that destroyed nearly the entire block of Green Street. Boone also owned the livery and Boone Stable in Bodie. *Historic American Buildings Survey, Library of Congress photos*

Below: The Bodie Railroad Station, photographed in 1932.

Lee Vining
Mono Lake

A highway sign (above) points the way to Mono Lake near Lee Vining (welcome sign, below), a former mining camp founded by Leroy Vining in 1852. Vining and his brother Richard returned to the area in 1857 and mined at Dog Town, now a ghost town just a little ways up the road. Three years later, he set up a sawmill and ranch near what would become Lee Vining Creek. When the town itself was laid out in 1926, it was called Lakeview, but the Postal Service demanded a change when it located a post office there two years later, because that name had already been taken. Lee Vining was eventually chosen. *Author photos*

Finding Lee Vining

Location: 25 miles south of Bridgeport on the western shore of Mono Lake near the State Route 120 junction to Yosemite; 30 miles north of Mammoth Lakes
Route: U.S. 395/Main Street

Above: This sketch of Mono Lake was included in Mark Twain's 1872 book, *Roughing It*. Twain wasn't particularly impressed by the lake, which he described as a "solemn, silent, sailless sea" and "this lonely tenant of the loneliest spot on earth." He continued: "There are no fish in Mono Lake—no frogs, no snakes, no polliwogs—nothing, in fact, that goes to make life desirable. Millions of wild ducks and sea-gulls swim about the surface, but no living thing exists *under* the surface, except a white feathery sort of worm, one half an inch long, which looks like a bit of white thread frayed out at the sides."

Left: A roadside plaque marks the grave of Adeline Carson Stilts, the daughter of Kit Carson, who "came to the gold site of 'Mono Diggins'' with her husband in about 1858." She died the following winter at the age of 21. The plaque is south of the Mono Inn but difficult to see if you're coming from the south because it's obscured by the tree at right. *Author photo*

Mono Inn, seen above in this 2023 author photo and featured in a 1957 ad at left, was built in 1921 as a bunkhouse.

FISHING ... HUNTING

Mono Inn

MONO LAKE ... CALIFORNIA
ON U. S. HIGHWAY 395, NORTH

Modern Cabins ... Store ... Gas
Off-Sale Liquors

FINE FOOD
Served by "Ted 'n Zella"...in the "Mono Diggins"

Cocktail Lounge ... Dining Room
OVERLOOKING BEAUTIFUL MONO LAKE

VENITA R. McPHERSON, Owner-Manager ... PHONE LEE VINING 2511

On the highway, 1922

"We were overnight at Mono Inn at western edge of Mono Lake; near this point starts the road over Tioga Pass to Yosemite Valley, 107 miles westward. Mono Lake at 6,400 feet is surely a beautiful body of water, and Mono Inn is a good place to stay overnight at reasonable rates. Tioga Lodge [is] someone finer and more expensive."

— McAllister and M.C.Z.,
Tulare Daily Advance, August 19

The restaurant and lobby of Tioga Lodge, on the east side of 395 north of Lee Vining, were built as a toll station, bar, and bordello in Bodie and moved to their current site around 1897. Canvas-covered summer cottages were added in 1920 after W.W. Cunningham bought the old J.P. Hammond homestead. *Author photos*

Left: In Lee Vining, you can stop at Mono Cone for soft-serve ice cream in a waffle cone, mozzarella sticks, a variety of burgers, or an Oreo shake.
Author photos

Right: Niceley's Restaurant has been open since 1965, serving up homestyle meals and diner food from seafood to steak to macaroni and cheese for the kids.

Silent film actress Nellie Bly O'Bryan led an interesting life. Named for famous journalist Nellie Bly, she began acting in motion pictures after meeting Charlie Chaplin, appearing in more than a dozen films during her career. But her real love was the outdoors, so she moved to Lundy Canyon, west of Mono Lake in the mid-1930s, where she built a cabin out of salvaged lumber from an old mining camp. .transformed it into the "Happy Landing Resort," complete with a store, restaurant, and cabins.

Outdoor enthusiasts new to the area began hiring her to help them explore, and she eventually became California's first woman to be licensed as a hunting and fishing guide. One day, she discovered a cabin that had tumbled down a hillside and landed upside-down at the bottom (above). It reminded her of a story she'd heard as a child, so she found furniture and decor, which she nailed to the floor and walls—upside down, just like the cabin. **Left:** 1957 ad for her business.

NELLIE BLY O'BRYAN
LICENSED FISHING AND HUNTING GUIDE

Let Me Plan Your Trip, and Take You into High Sierra Back Country
FOR
FISHING AND HUNTING

23 years of experience in the High Sierras. I have fished over 1000 lakes. Guide service includes camping equipment, planning of meals, all camp work. Will take you where you want to go or will select spot for you. Reasonable rates.

FOR FURTHER INFORMATION, WRITE:
NELLIE BLY O'BRYAN, MONO LAKE, CALIF.
Contact at Mono Inn, on U. S. 395, North of Lee Vining

The Lee Vining Motel's office and neon sign, above, occupy a former service station and canopied bay in town. At right, a vertical sign that indicates when there's a vacancy at the motel next door. *Author photos*

On the highway, 1920

"The 'going' over the desert for eight or nine miles north of Mono Lake, or Tioga Lodge, is a little better this season than it has been in previous years, but even at that driving in the sand channels, if a speed of more than ten miles per hour is maintained, will toss passengers around considerably."
— *San Francisco Chronicle, July 18*

The Tioga Gas and Gift Mart just west of the 120 junction is more than a Mobil station. It's got a gourmet restaurant inside called the Whoa Nellie Deli. You order at the counter, but the food is far from conventional minimart fare. Hudson Sangree wrote for the *Los Angeles Times* in 2002: "To have one of the better meals of your life in a gas station is bizarre. It leaves you staring at your plate for a moment or two in disbelief." *Author photos*

Mono Lake looking north from Lee Vining. *Author photo*

Getting there, 1918

Directions from Bridgeport heading south to Mono Lake on El Camino Sierra, according to the 1918 Automobile Blue Book, with miles between each entry:

0.3 miles: Fork just beyond small wooden bridge; bear right.

2.2 miles: Fork; bear left with travel.

2.8 miles: Fork, cabin in center; bear left. Pass county farm.

5.1 miles: Fork; bear left.

0.3 miles: Fork, sign in center; bear right.

6.7 miles: Right-hand diagonal road; bear right with poles.

3.8 miles: Prominent fork, sign in center; bear left.

3.9 miles: Fork; bear left along fence.

0.9 miles: Fork, small wooden school in center; bear left. Pass Mono Lake P.O. on left. Thru Hammond.

DETOUR ▶ June Lake

June Lake is the highlight of the June Lake Loop, a roughly five-mile detour west of 395 that drops you back out on the highway when you're done. *Author photo*

Left: The Frank Sam Cabin near the June Lake Loop turnoff was built in the 1920s and occupied until the early '60s.

The June Lake Loop leads to three other lakes: Gull Lake, Silver Lake, and the largest, Grant Lake. Several bars and taverns opened around June Lake, such as Glen Colton's Tiger Bar in 1932, Bud Kline's Tavern (with its motto, "Once a fisherman—always a liar") and Bill's Grill ("where sportsmen meet for fun"). With the liquor flowing and workers streaming in for the Mono Basin Project in the 1930s, an appetite grew for gambling, and several of the bars installed illegal slot machines. According to legend, many of these one-armed bandits were dumped into June Lake when word spread that State Revenue Agents were on their way. Since then, several dive teams have tried, unsuccessfully, to find and retrieve them. *Author photos*

Above: This photo from a 1957 advertisement shows Siler's June Lake Garage, owned by John Siler, which dispensed Mobil products.

Below: Ads for Bill's Grill and Ernie's Tackle & Gift Shop,1963.

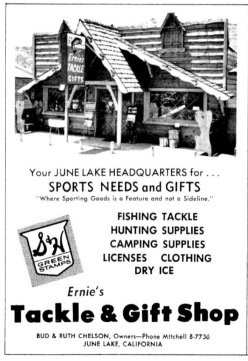

June Lake Junction, seen in this 1957 ad and two author photos from 2023, was founded in 1926 by former Standard Oil mechanic Guy Rarick Carrington, who had come to the area to work for W.W. Cunningham at Tioga Lodge. The place went by several names, including Carrington's and Crater Garage.

The June Lake Villager Motel was built in 1926, but it wasn't the first inn at the lake. A tent camp called Carson's first welcomed tourists in 1920 and added two cabins the following year. Others such as Fern Creek Lodge and Camp Culver soon followed.

Above: The June Lake Market and General Store was in business by 1951, with owners Lloyd and Dorris Burris offering "the most complete stock of vacation needs in all the High Sierras," according to a May 30 ad in the *Los Angeles Daily News*. Competitor Louie's Market & Bakery, owned by trucker Louis Prole and his wife, Pauline, until 1977, offered the "lowest prices in all the Sierras" and had been in business since 1932.

Following page: 1957 ad for June Lake General Store.

Finding June Lake

Location: 11 miles south of Lee Vining; 18 miles north of Mammoth Lakes

Route: State Route 158/June Lake Loop

> END DETOUR

Mammoth Lakes

Above: A village street at Mammoth, with a gas station at left and Lutz Grocery on the right, c. the 1920s. The area now known as Old Mammoth included the Sierra Café, Mammoth Saloon, a Standard station and Navajo Johnson's Trading post. The Lutz store took over a store owned by Charles Summers, who had started out with a hotel there in 1918. Summers sold gas, but via a one-gallon hand pump. *Author collection*

Right: Mammoth Liquor on SR 203. *Author photo*

Finding Mammoth Lakes

Location: 30 miles south of Lee Vining and Mono Lake;
42 miles northwest of Bishop
Route: State Route 203/Main Street, a few miles west of 395

Heading south on 395 in the Mammoth Lakes area. *Author photo*

Above: State Route 203 heading west toward Mammoth Lakes. Just nine miles long, it originally went to Lake Mary before the route was shifted toward Mammoth Ski Area.

Left: U.S. 395 heading south toward the 203 junction. *Author photos*

Left: Businesses along the Route 203 frontage road in Mammoth include a Shell service station and Schat's Bakery & Café, open since the early 1970s there and since 1938 at its first location in Bishop. *Author photo*

On the highway, 1980

"A series of strong earthquakes Sunday jolted the Mammoth Lakes area on the eastern slope of the Sierra Nevada, triggering rock slides as far as 50 miles away and swaying buildings from Sacramento to Los Angeles… Highway 395, the major north-south roadway along the eastern slope, remained open to fleeing tourists although it showed some cracks and was covered in spots by rocks, said a dispatcher for the state Office of Emergency Services."

— *Sacramento Bee, May 26*

Left: Skiers and snowboarders gather atop Mammoth Mountain. The ski area began in 1941 when snow surveyor Dave McCoy got a permit for a portable rope tow there. He'd been operating one down the road at McGee Mountain off 395 since 1938 but found the snow there wasn't heavy enough. The first permanent tow at Mammoth came in 1945, and he later built a small lodge. McCoy built the first chairlift there in 1955.

Below: A mammoth statue at the lodge. *Author photos*

Above: Open pits called the Inyo Craters are part of a volcanic chain in a forested area north of Mammoth Lakes, accessible via an unpaved road off the Mammoth Scenic Loop. *U.S. Geological Survey*

Left: Obsidian Dome, seen here in 2022, lies to the north, west of 395 and south of June Lake. The dome erupted in the mid-14th century. The Mammoth area continues to experience seismic activity. *Author photos*

Right: Devil's Postpile National Monument is a collection of column-shaped basalt formations, more than half of which have hexagonal shapes. The monument is accessible by shuttle from the Mammoth Mountain Main Lodge parking lot. *California State University, Chico, Meriam Library Special Collections*

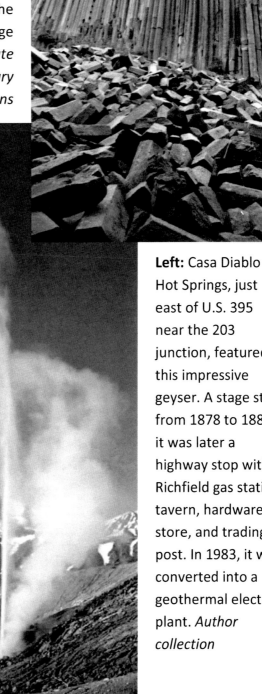

Left: Casa Diablo Hot Springs, just east of U.S. 395 near the 203 junction, featured this impressive geyser. A stage stop from 1878 to 1881, it was later a highway stop with a Richfield gas station, tavern, hardware store, and trading post. In 1983, it was converted into a geothermal electric plant. *Author collection*

Directions from Mono Lake to Diablo Hot Springs heading south, according to the 1918 Automobile Blue Book, with miles between each entry:

5.1 miles: Fork; bear left with travel across bridge over creek (and) thru ford.

1.1 miles: Pass farm house on left keeping ahead thru flat prairie, crossing numerous irrigation ditches.

3.0 miles: Pass Farrington's Ranch on right. Pass Caine Ranch on left (1.1 miles later), keeping ahead thru ford.

1.5 miles: End of road, at cabin; turn left across small bridge.

2.7 miles: Right-hand diagonal road, two lone pine trees just ahead; bear right away from travel going upgrade.

1.9 miles: End of road; turn right.

0.2 miles: Fork; bear right. Under power line.

1.8 miles: Fork; bear right.

0.7 miles: End of road; turn left with travel. Pass Devils Punch Bowl on right.

5.3 miles: Under power lines. Go down grade, using extreme caution for hairpin turns over Dead Man's Hill, keeping ahead with travel.

5.4 miles: Fork, sign "Mammoth" in center; bear left.

5.7 miles: Casa Diablo Hot Springs, cabin on right. Keep ahead.

SIERRA HIGHWAY

If you keep going beyond Mammoth Mountain Ski Area, you'll come to Minarets Vista at the end of the road. The jagged peaks were named the Minarets, above, by the California Geographical Survey in 1868. Seventeen have unofficial names honoring local explorers. They're part of the Ritter Range.
Author photos

Overlooking Twin Lakes from Lake Mary Road in 2023. If you're driving west on SR 203 and turn right (north) onto Minaret Road, it will take you to the ski lodge. If you keep going straight on Lake Mary Road, however, you'll find yourself at Twin Lakes and Tamarack Lodge. *Author photo*

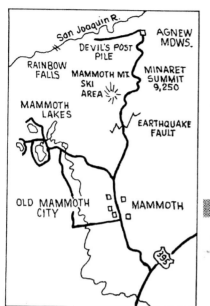

Vaudeville actor and comedian Eddie Foy, who performed with his family and children "The Seven Little Foys," built Tamarack Lodge (seen below in a 1955 ad) in 1924. Nearly a century later, it's the oldest continuously operating lodge in Mammoth Lakes.

Tamarack Lodge
On Beautiful Twin Lakes

Trout Fishing . . . Boating . . . Evening Entertainment
Scenic Trails for Hiking or Riding

FORTY CLEAN, MODERN HOUSEKEEPING CABINS
LODGE ROOMS . . . WITH OR WITHOUT BATH

Mr. and Mrs. D. E. McGuffin

SUMMER ADDRESS: MAMMOTH LAKES, CALIF.
WINTER ADDRESS: 1722 HILLIARD DR., SAN MARINO, CALIF.

Recreation on Lake Mamie, above, and Horseshoe Lake, right, in 2023. These are two of the four lakes on upper Lake Mary Road, joining Lake Mary and Lake George. All are at elevations of about 9,000 feet. *Author photo*

SIERRA HIGHWAY

Waterfall full of
spring runoff
emptying into Twin
Lakes, from above
(right) and below.
Author photos

The Hot Creek Geological Site is one of several hots springs near Mammoth. Although the waters are not open to the public, it's free to look. Part of the Long Valley Caldera, an oval volcanic depression bisected by 395, it's about 10 miles east of Mammoth Lakes: Go south on 395 and take Hot Creek Hatchery Road east to the overlook. Other hot springs in the area (where you *can* enjoy the waters) include Whitmore and Wild Willy's Crowley Hot Springs. Like Hot Creek, they're both northeast of 395, but a little farther south. *Author photo*

A sign on U.S. 395 North at Pearsonville informs motorists they're entering Inyo County, "The Heart of El Camino Sierra." *Author photo*

Inyo County
Bishop to Inyokern   127 miles

Inyo County was in many ways the birthplace of U.S. 395, with the Inyo Good Road secretary W. Scott Gilette spearheading the movement for the Pasear Tour and the creation of the Sierra Highway. Scott's influence in the county was significant as manager of the Inyo Mines Syndicate, and he brought that influence to bear in advocating for improved roads in the region.

His efforts weren't limited to the Sierra Highway, either. He also spoke out on behalf of the Midland Trail, serving as vice president of the association promoting that road.

A coast-to-coast road like the Lincoln Highway, the Midland Trail wound down from Salt Lake City into eastern Nevada in Ely before following the path of later U.S. Highway 6 from there to Tonopah. It then curved south to just past Goldfield—the early 20ᵗʰ century Central Nevada boomtown—before veering west again at Lida Junction, following Nevada Highway 266 across the state line.

Its route to the Sierra Highway took it through the White Mountains to Big Pine via the Westgard Pass on what's now California State Route 168. There, the Midland Trail split in two, heading both north and south along the Sierra Highway, with the northern branch ending in San Francisco, and the southern branch in Los Angeles.

(Note: SR 168 follows the northern route from Big Pine to Bishop along U.S. 395 before turning west again and hitting a dead end at Lake Sabrina. It's a peculiar highway in that it picks up again on the other side of the Sierra at Huntington Lake, descending the foothills into Fresno. The Sierra "gap" between the two sections exists because 168 was originally conceived as a trans-Sierra highway... but never completed.)

On the highway, 1913

"The 'Midland Trail,' third of the three transcontinental routes to be laid out this year by A.A.A. Touring Information Board, is now in the process of preparation, with A.L. Westgard, the association's field representative, well on his way from New York to Los Angeles..."
— *Tonopah Daily Bonanza, October 22*

Carving out a highway over the White Mountains wasn't easy: A one-lane "cut" through the mountains east of Big Pine testifies to the difficulty road workers faced. Nevertheless, the highway finally met up with El Camino Sierra (later U.S. 395) at Big Pine in 1913, and a giant Sequioa tree was planted at the junction, honoring Teddy Roosevelt and commemorating the feat.

Above: Stump of the Roosevelt Tree and a marker at the junction of the Midland Trail and El Camino Sierra in Big Pine.

Right: Highway sign in the White Mountains on State Route 168. Author photos

HAZARD GARAGE - BISHOP

Service Station—General Repairing—Tires—Accessories—"The Garage where Tourists get their fishing and other information and make their headquarters."

The stump of the tree and historical markers can still be found at that junction, but other early remnants of the Sierra Highway are long gone.

W.G. Scott wasn't the only auto trail pioneer to leave his mark on the future 395. Another important Inyo County resident was Lemoyne Hazard, a sheriff's deputy who also happened to own Hazard's Garage in Bishop, which sold Shell gasoline, serviced Buicks, and offered tires, tubes, and accessories for Dodge Brothers cars.

"We know the requirements of the tourist and are PREPARED TO TAKE CARE OF THEM," one ad read. That didn't mean just providing automobile service, but maps and information about where to camp, hunt... and fish. A 1926 ad in the *Los Angeles Times* (below) touted Hazard's as "The Garage where Tourists get their fishing and other information and make their headquarters."

A large, fish-shaped sign emblazoned with Hazard's name surmounted the canopy at the Bishop station at the corner of Main (future 395) and Lagoon streets.

Fishing was a big deal in the Eastern Sierra, and Lemoyne Hazard knew that all too well. The new Sierra Highway was a great new way to travel, and Hazard wanted to help sportsmen find their way to the best camping spots and fishing holes (and, of course, to his garage). To that end, he published maps and a magazine called *Dreamalog*, and he put up signs on the Sierra Highway and Midland Trail that showed the distance to various towns and points of interest.

In keeping with the region's fishing theme, these distinctive red signs were shaped like, well, a fish. A photo from the 1910s shows one of the signs, on the Midland Trail in Utah, with distances to Ely (60-some miles), the California state line (334 miles), Bishop & Owens Valley (370-plus miles), and Los Angeles (667 miles).

Other signs gave fishermen tips about where to fish. One warned that there was "positively no fishing allowed in this lake" and suggested that motorists "come on to Bishop and we'll show you where to get 'em."

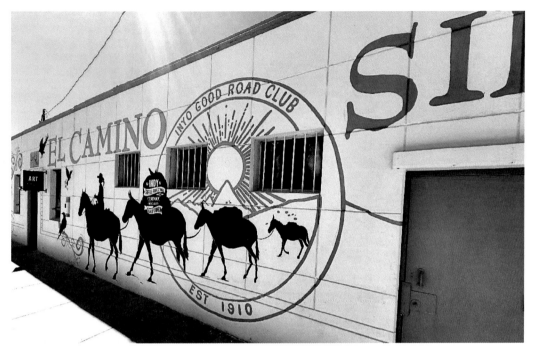

A mural on Lagoon Street at Main—the same intersection where Hazard's once stood—celebrates El Camino Sierra and the Inyo Good Road Club. *Author photo*

Unfortunately, Lemoyne Hazard didn't live to see his labor bear the kind of fruit he might have wished. His other occupation, as a deputy sheriff was a dangerous one, and it proved his tragic undoing in January of 1925, when he tried to arrest a man named Charlie Jackson, described in a press account as a "whiskey-crazed" Native American.

Jackson shot Hazard and a companion with a rifle, then used the stock of the weapon to smash his head in—which proved to be the ultimate cause of death.

Hazard was just 46 years old.

Hazard's Garage continued to operate, under new ownership, at least into the early 1930s, but the red fish signs, like the old Burma-Shave markers, are long gone.

Tom's Place

Tom's Place isn't a town but a resort. Still, it's listed on official California roadside mileage signs because it's an institution. Tom and Hazel Yerby built the original Tom's Place, north of Bishop, in 1923, adding a lodge, cabins, a store and café to the old Rock Creek Station. Tom Yerby died in 1940, and Hazel ran the place for five more years. It burned down in 1947, and the new owners rebuilt it.

WATER
COURTESY OF
TOMS PLACE GARAGE
TOWING   REPAIRS
DO NOT DRINK

Always at Your Service!

...No doubt you have seen this welcome sight—our water-tank trailer— parked near the top of Sherwin Grade north of Bishop during the summer months. Always full of water, it has often proved quite helpful to hundreds of cars making this steep climb. If you need further service on your car, we will be glad to help you.

Towing-Repairing

TOM'S PLACE
GARAGE
TOM'S PLACE, CALIFORNIA
ON U. S. HIGHWAY 395

Author photo top; ad from 1956 above, postcard left (author collection)

The junction of U.S. 6 and U.S. 395 at the north end of Bishop. U.S. 6 ends here, but it once shared the road with 395 down to Bradys, where it veered west again through Mojave to its ultimate destination in Long Beach. *Author photo*

Bishop

County: Inyo

Elevation: 4,150

Established: 1861

Incorporated: 1903

    1920 — Population: 1,304

    2020 — Population: 3,819

Key buildings on 395:

    Depot, Laws RR Museum (1883)

    Bishop Theatre (1929)

    Erick Schat's Bakkery (1938)

    Downtown district

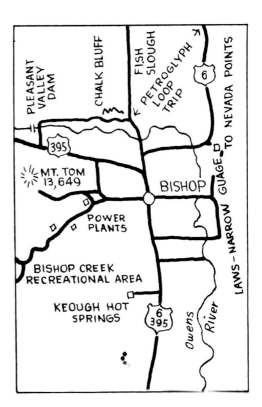

By the time you get to Tom's Place, you're at the gateway to Inyo County, and that resort marks a transition of sorts from the High Sierra portion of U.S. 395 to the lower elevations of Inyo County as you head south into the Mojave Desert.

The highway runs over the western edge of that famed desert starting a little south of Bishop—with the famed Death Valley off to the east of Independence and Lone Pine—all the way south to Inyokern. The descent from Mono County over Sherwin Grade is a dramatic one, dropping from over 7,000 feet at Tom's Place down to barely 4,100 at Bishop: nearly 3,000 feet in a space of just 24 miles.

Bishop was founded in 1861 as a cattle town to supply beef for the mining boomtown of Aurora, Nevada, about 120 miles to the north. That might seem like a long trip, but before that, cattlemen had driven their herds nearly three times as far from the Central Valley across the Sierra at Walker Pass. It was much easier, they found, to settle in the fertile Owens Valley and raise their cattle there.

Samuel Addison Bishop was one of those cattlemen, arriving in the summer of 1861 with his family and hired men as they led about 600 head of cattle and 50 horses from Fort Tejon in the Tehachapi Mountains. When he reached the Owens Valley, he built a ranch and established a meat market catering to miners and residents of Aurora.

Business must have been good, because by 1863, Aurora was teeming with as many as 10,000 people—more than twice the population of Bishop today. It was even the seat of Mono County for a brief time, until surveyors discovered it wasn't in California, but Nevada. Its heyday, however, was brief. By 1870 the boom was fading and half the town's houses were deserted.

Bishop, on the other hand, endured. In 1862, more settlers came and established a settlement called Bishop Creek a couple of miles from Samuel Bishop's homestead. It was in Tulare County at the time but became part of Inyo County when that jurisdiction was created in 1866. (The town's name was eventually shortened to Bishop.)

Ads from the mid-1950s for businesses on U.S. Highways 6 and 395 in Bishop.

During the age of the automobile, Bishop became Inyo County's largest—and only incorporated—city. No other Inyo County town along 395 has a population of more than 2,100, and as of 2023, the county seat of Independence didn't even have as many as 700.

Bishop itself was never a metropolis by any stretch of the imagination, but it stood at an important crossroads where the transcontinental U.S. Highway 6 funneled motorists in from the east onto the Three Flags Highway, U.S. 395.

U.S. 6, also known as the Grand Army of the Republic Highway, was actually the longest highway in the country: For 28 years, beginning in 1936, it ran from Massachusetts southwest all the way to Long Beach, California. Before the highways were renumbered in 1964, it shared the road with 395 from Bishop south to Bradys, a highway stop near Inyokern, a distance of about 130 miles. Many ads for service stations and diners along this stretch touted the fact that they were on both 6 and 395.

Today, however, U.S. 6 stops at the north end of Bishop, and if you're heading east, you can take it to Tonopah, Nevada.

The Bishop Drive-In made its debut in 1956 with one screen and room for 460 cars. Its last advertisement in the *Los Angeles Times* appeared in April of 1963.

On the highway, 1957

"If you have visited Inyo-Mono before, you will undoubtedly remember driving over the Sherwin Grade [above, author photo], about 15 miles north of Bishop on U.S. 395. This stretch of Road, a series of curves, switchbacks, and steep climbs has always been a time-consuming as well as dangerous part of the highway, especially during the summer months when slow-moving trucks and house trailers make its passage long and tedious. And it is no bargain in winter, either, when snow and ice have often made it dangerous.'

"So, it will certainly be good news to you—that this 12-mile stretch of dangerous and outdated road has been eliminated from U.S. Highway 395. And it is replaced with a fine new, modern road which not only eliminates practically all the turns, but has a maximum of six percent grade..."

— *Inyo-Mono Fishing and Vacation Guide*

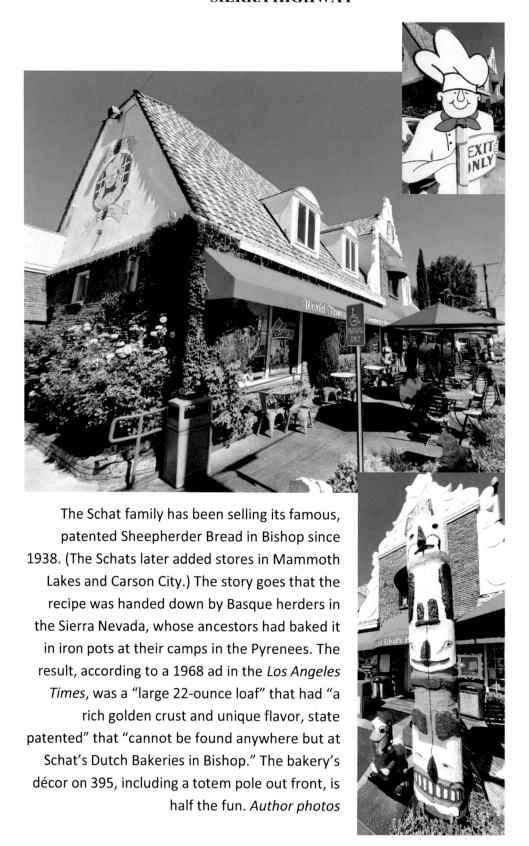

The Schat family has been selling its famous, patented Sheepherder Bread in Bishop since 1938. (The Schats later added stores in Mammoth Lakes and Carson City.) The story goes that the recipe was handed down by Basque herders in the Sierra Nevada, whose ancestors had baked it in iron pots at their camps in the Pyrenees. The result, according to a 1968 ad in the *Los Angeles Times*, was a "large 22-ounce loaf" that had "a rich golden crust and unique flavor, state patented" that "cannot be found anywhere but at Schat's Dutch Bakeries in Bishop." The bakery's décor on 395, including a totem pole out front, is half the fun. *Author photos*

DAY *and*
NIGHT
SUMMER *and*
WINTER

Tony's Union 76 station was a fixture in Bishop for years. It had already been in business for 37 years when the ad at left appeared in 1957, and it was still in business 14 years later when the photo at top was taken. *Suzanne Edmonds, Creative Commons, cinematreasures*

CONTINUOUS SERVICE FOR THE PAST 37 YEARS

- FREE MAPS... ROAD INFORMATION
- CLEAN RESTROOMS
- FISHING AND HUNTING INFORMATION

SERVICE STATION

ON HIGHWAYS 6 & 395 • DOWNTOWN BISHOP • KEN JOHNSON, OWNER

A number of vintage motels
still operate along U.S. 395
and nearby as of 2023.
Author photos

Left: Ben Franklin five-and-dime stores were once common sights across the country, but it's rare to see one nowadays. This sign is on the highway in downtown Bishop. *Author photos*

Above: This mural shows the Kittie Lee Inn, which for years was the destination of choice for well-to-do Eastern Sierra visitors, including the Hollywood set. Matt Wilkinson opened the establishment on Main Street (later U.S. 395) in 1924, naming it for his daughter. The Copper Kettle Restaurant and Charlie's Room Bar were added in 1946, but the inn was demolished in 1965. *Author photos, 1952 L.A. Daily News ad for the Kittie Lee below*

KITTIE LEE INN & COPPER KETTLE COFFEE SHOP
Bishop. Ph. 2641. "It's New Again." Newly renovated—completely modernized—phone in every room. The Owens Valley's
Really Fine Hotel.

On the highway, 1926

"The Kittie Lee Inn at Bishop, the gateway to the High Sierras, is a most convenient starting point for side trips to the many beautiful lakes close at hand... The inn has 55 rooms with baths; everything is spic and span as well as modern, and it has a good reputation for quality of service and cuisine. A unique feature of the inn is its spacious lobby, where a pool has been installed, in which trout play around."

— *Los Angeles Evening Express, May 21*

U.S. 395 through Bishop as it appeared in the 1940s. Notice Tony's 76 station at right in the foreground. *Suzanne Edmonds, Creative Commons, cinematreasures*

Finding Bishop

Location: 42 miles southeast of Mammoth Lakes; 15 miles north of Big Pine

Route: U.S. 395 and former U.S. 6/Main Street

The 400-seat Bishop Theatre, now a duplex, opened in 1929, replacing the former Holland's Opera House and Bishop Theatre, which had burned down five years earlier. *Author photo*

Big Pine

Above: Big Pine High School was built in 1921, and soon became embroiled in controversy. Two years later, Alice Piper, 15, a Paiute girl living in town, wanted to attend the high school rather than a separate "Indian school." Her parents sued the school district, claiming separate schools for Native Americans were unconstitutional. In 1924, the state Supreme Court ruled unanimously in their favor because her father was a taxpaying citizen. Piper's case was later used as precedent in the landmark desegregation ruling, Brown v. Board of Education. The 1924 ruling is memorialized in a plaque and the statue seen above in front of the school on U.S. 395.

Below: Businesses along 395 in Big Pine, 2023. *Author photos*

We Are Conveniently Near

Excellent Trout Fishing
Good Deer and Bird Hunting
Breathtaking Scenery

Why not make Glacier View Motel your headquarters while you are visiting in the Inyo-Mono
region? You'll find its accommodations clean and
comfortable. The location is superb, and every
cabin is air conditioned in summer and heated in
the winter. Convenient to fishing and hunting.
Rates Are Reasonable.

Clean, Comfortable Cottages
COOLED IN SUMMER . . . HEATED IN WINTER

JIM NIKOLAUS

'Near the Famous Palisade Glacier'
TELEPHONE 206 · BIG PINE, CALIF.

Overnight options past and present for travelers in Big Pine (2020 population: 1,875). The Starlight Motel, across from the high school, opened in 1950. Ed Hall, a power plant operator, moved to Big Pine in 1944 and used his engineering skills to design the Big Pine Motel in his spare time. The Glacier View offered 11 modern units, with rates of $4 for a double-bed unit or $4.50 for twin beds. *Author photos, 1957 ad*

Finding Big Pine

Location: 15 miles south of Bishop; 26 miles north of Independence
Route: U.S. 395 and former U.S. 6/Main Street

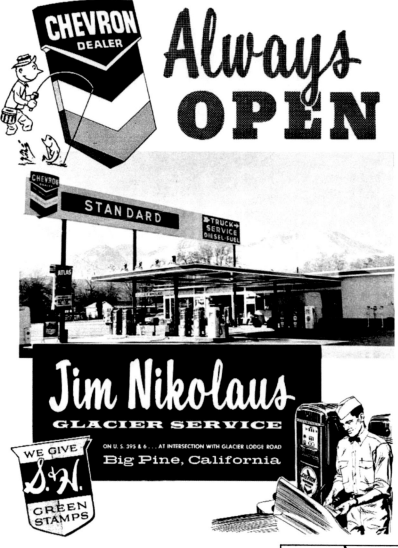

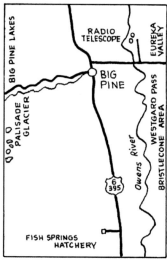

The Jim Nikolaus Glacier Service station is seen in this 1962 fishing guide ad. Although it was touted in 1957 as "one of Inyo-Mono's newest and largest service stations, Nikolaus had been in business for at least 10 years by then at U.S. 395 and Glacier Lodge Road. Nikolaus was also invested in talc deposits (which he sold in 1951), and in the mid-1960s served as president of the Big Pine Civic Club. There were still Chevron and Shell service stations at that intersection in 2023.

The Ancient Bristlecone Pine Forest lies about 24 miles northeast of Big Pine off State Route 168. The forest in the White Mountains grows at about 10,000 feet above sea level and includes the Methuselah tree, the world's oldest confirmed non-cloned organism at nearly 4,900 years of age.

Independence

Despite its small size (around 700 people), Independence has been the seat of Inyo County since its creation in 1866. It almost wasn't, though. The mining town of Kearsarge was considered a favorite for the honor, but the mine was buried under an avalanche that same year, and much of the population moved to Independence. The courthouse above was built in 1922. *Author photo*

Finding Independence

Location: 26 miles south of Big Pine; 9 miles north of Manzanar and 16 miles north of Lone Pine

Route: U.S. 395 and former U.S. 6/ Edwards Street

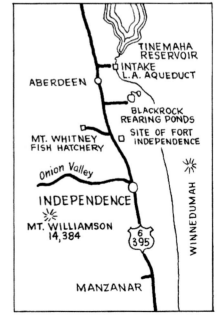

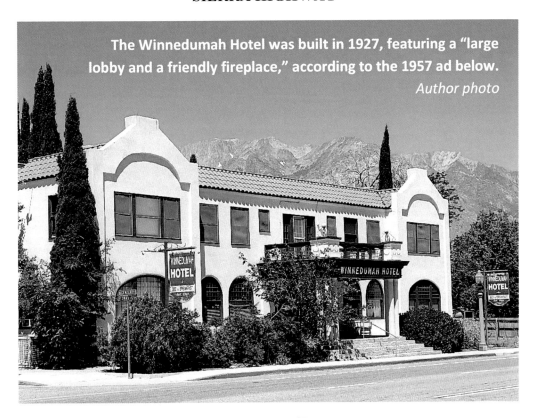

The Winnedumah Hotel was built in 1927, featuring a "large lobby and a friendly fireplace," according to the 1957 ad below.
Author photo

On the highway, 1928

"But one hotel in the country can claim the distinction of having in its back yard—as it were—a majestic, snow-covered mountain measuring over 14,000 feet. This hostelry is the Winnedumah Hotel at Independence, Inyo County, where Mount Whitney... makes it a mecca to those who admire the staunch, rugged crags of the high Sierras... It is practically new, luxuriously furnished and steam-heated; every room has hot and cold water. There is a big lobby with a unique fireplace and cosy, colorful music rooms."

you'll enjoy your stay at the
Winnedumah Hotel
Conveniently Located in Downtown Independence

LUXURIOUSLY FURNISHED . . . STEAM HEATED
EVERY ROOM WITH RUNNING HOT AND COLD WATER
LARGE LOBBY AND FRIENDLY FIREPLACE

WINNEDUMAH HOTEL
INDEPENDENCE, CALIF.   FRED A. SCHAEFER, Prop.

— *Los Angeles Evening Express, May 21*

Once upon a time, the Pines Café served up "good food at reasonable prices" 24 hours a day. In the 1940s, a sporting goods and hardware store occupied one corner of the building, with the Pines in the other half. The owners of the store lived upstairs for about six months before moving their business across the street, making way for a Post Office (which eventually moved as well, leaving the entire building to the Pines). The café served complete dinners, including charcoal broiled steaks and chops. Unfortunately, the Pines closed in 2004 and was still boarded up when this photo was taken in 2022. *Author photo*

WELCOME! TRAVELER!

To The

PINES CAFE

In

Independence

Gateway to some of the best fishing and hunting in the High Sierras.

We're Open 24 Hours A Day

To Serve You

Good Food

At Reasonable Prices!

Open Seven Days A Week

PINES CAFE

Mr. and Mrs. Clyde O'Harra
106 SOUTH EDWARDS
Independence

Above: Author Mary Hunter Austin once lived just a few blocks west of Highway 395 in this home at 253 Market Street in Independence. Austin began writing in 1900, with her first published works being a series of essays about the Owens Valley, and her first book three years later, *The Land of Little Rain*, portraying the beauty of the desert valley. Austin and her then-husband, Wallace Austin, designed the home in Independence, which she left in 1906 to move to Carmel-by-the-Sea. It was there that she became part of a circle that included the likes of Jack London, Ambrose Bierce, and Sinclair Lewis. *Author photos*

Right: Historical landmark with a quote from The Land of Little Rain: "But if ever you come beyond the borders as far as the town that lies in a hill dimple at the foot of Kearsarge, never leave it until you have knocked at the door of the brown house under the willow-tree at the end of the village street..."

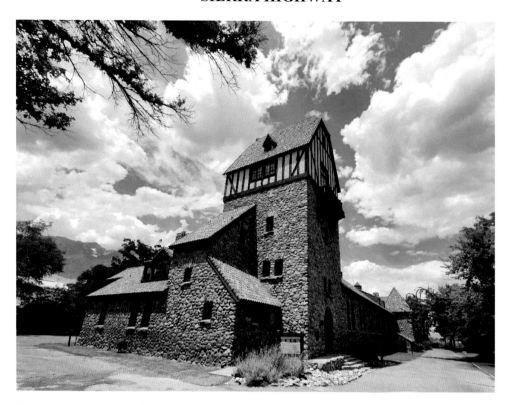

The Mount Whitney Fish Hatchery just outside of Independence, about a mile west of 395, was built using 3,500 tons of granite. The citizens of Independence raised $1,500 toward construction. When completed for $60,000 in 1917, it was the largest hatchery in the state and could produce 2 million fish fry per year. *Author photos*

Manzanar

Manzanar was once a small town on U.S. 395, but became infamous during World War II as the site of an internment camp (technically called a "war relocation center") where Japanese Americans were held against their will.

The town of Manzanar, founded in 1905, grew to include more than 25 homes, a general store, school, and town hall by 1920, with residents earning a living by farming nearly 5,000 acres of fruit trees, potatoes, corn, alfalfa, and other crops. But when Los Angeles began diverting water from the Owens River to water new subdivisions in the San Fernando Valley, the area dried up, and the town was all but abandoned by 1929: The last resident, a poultry farmer, left in 1935. These photos from 2022 are from the site of the internment camp. The entrance stations above are original construction. *Author photos*

Manzanar before the WRA camp: Manzanar Community Hall (top), seen around 1912, housed Hatfield's (later Bandhauer's) General Store and the town post office. The house above was owned by John Kispert, who established a ranch where he planted barley to sell to miners in 1861, a year after a stage stop was created there. *Library of Congress photos*

Top: Barracks at Manzanar in 1943. The camp, which operated from March 1942 to November 1945, housed more than 11,000 Japanese Americans along with 400 War Relocation Authority workers and their families. *Ansel Adams, Library of Congress*

Above: Re-created scene inside barracks at Manzanar (Spanish for "apple orchard"), 2022. *Author photo*

Softball, baseball, and basketball were popular pastimes at Manzanar and in other internment camps, providing the illusion of normalcy amid the harsh conditions and bitter reality of captivity. *Dorothea Lange, Library of Congress top; author photo above*

Above: Internees were expected to work fields that had been abandoned by others after Owens Valley water was siphoned off via aqueduct to Los Angeles. *Ansel Adams, Library of Congress*

Below: Communal toilets such as this one offered no privacy. *Author photo*

Finding Manzanar

Location: 9 miles south of Independence; 7 miles north of Lone Pine

Route: U.S. 395 and former U.S. 6

Manzanar had its own newspaper, the *Free Press*, published by internees. The first issue was published on April 11, 1942. *Dorothea Lange, Library of Congress*

But life at Manzanar was anything but free: Guard towers were a constant reminder of the internees' confinement, and tensions boiled over in early December of 1942, when 500 men came together outside the police station to demand the release of activist Harry Ueno—accused in beating a rumored FBI informant the night before. When they refused to disperse and some in the crowd began throwing rocks at the station, police responded by hurling tear gas at the protestors. Some in the crowd began to flee, but as the gas stung their eyes, they lost their sense of direction and ran *toward* the police lines. Two officers began shooting, killing two of the protestors and injuring nine others. *Author photos*

Above: The auditorium at Manzanar, an original building from the camp, once hosted concerts, dances, movies, lectures, talent shows and athletic events. Its 14,000 square feet had room for 1,280 seats, locker rooms, and a projection booth. Tickets for social events such as movies and dances were a quarter for adults and a nickel for kids. Today, the building serves as a visitor center. The National Park Service purchased it in 1996 and spent $3.5 million to rehabilitate it.

Right: Manzanar Cemetery. *Author photos*

Entering Lone Pine from the north on U.S. 395, with the Mt. Whitney Motel at right. The 15-unit motel was open by 1949, when it was advertised as the only motel in town. Lone Pine's population then was 1,415, and it has grown modestly since then to 2,014 at the 2020 census. *Author photo*

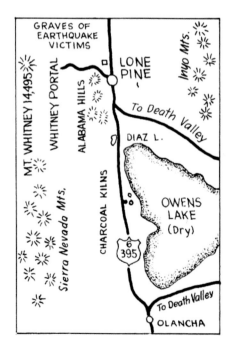

Finding Lone Pine

Location: 7 miles south of Manzanar; about 20 miles north of Cartago

Route: U.S. 395 and former U.S. 6/Main Street

Sleep in the Shadow of Mt. Whitney

At the Famous

DOW HOTEL

First Air-Conditioned Hotel
In The West

Telephones in Every Room

65 ROOMS
$4 to $8

GEORGE BOWSER, Manager

DOW
hotel
LONE PINE, CALIF

PHONE LONE PINE 2281 . . . OR WRITE FOR RESERVATIONS

The Dow was the hotel that Hollywood built: It was established in 1923 to serve movie crews who arrived to film westerns and other features in the nearby Alabama Hills. Gene Autry, Errol Flynn, John Wayne, Robert Mitchum, William Boyd, and other stars have all stayed there. The original hotel had 20 rooms and was later expanded to 50. The adjacent Dow Villa Motel was added in 1959. *Author photo*

The neon sign at Margie's Merry Go Round Restaurant in Lone Pine is one of the most distinctive you're likely to find. The place has been there since the 1950s, and the menu offers an array of choices from egg fu young, tofu, and fried rice to pasta, ribs, lamb, and even shrimp enchiladas. *Author photo*

Other distinctive neon signs in Lone Pine harken back to an earlier time and reflect the love of fishing in the area.
Author photos

Top: Frosty Chalet has been open at the north end of town since at least the 1960s. *Author photos*

Above: The Museum of Western Film History was founded in 2006 and documents the film industry's legacy in Lone Pine and the surrounding area. Since the first location shoot in Lone Pine (Fatty Arbuckle's silent Western *The Round Up* in 1920), scenes from more than 400 feature films have been shot there, in the Alabama Hills, Owens Valley, and nearby Sierra.

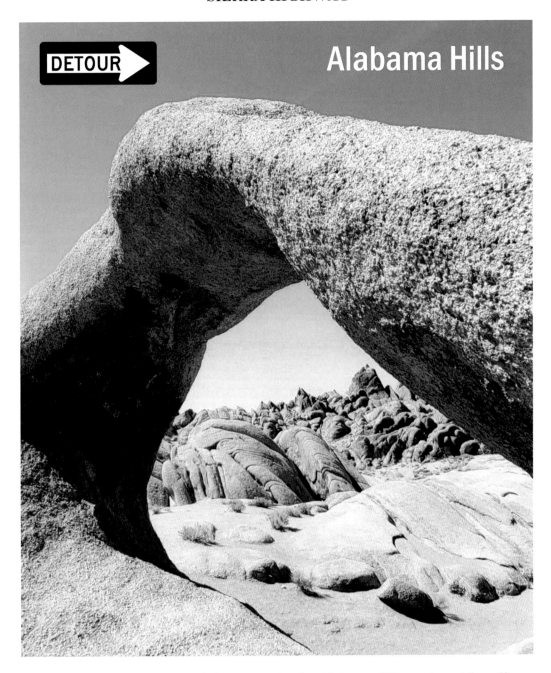

DETOUR ▶ Alabama Hills

You can find the Mobius Arch formation in the Alabama Hills, a short hike off the road. The hills are, of course, nowhere near Alabama. Southern sympathizers in the Civil War era coined the name to celebrate the exploits of a Confederate cruiser named the Alabama, which reportedly sank or captured more than 60 Union ships. When the Alabama was sunk itself by the U.S.S. Kearsarge in 1864, Union sympathizers near Independence retaliated by naming their mining claims Kearsarge. *Author photos*

Finding Alabama Hills

Location: About 7 miles west of Lone Pine off U.S. 395
Route: Whitney Portal Road

More rock formations from the Alabama Hills, which proved to be an ideal location for Hollywood film shoots. A dozen John Wayne films were shot in Movie Flats, while stars such as Clint Eastwood, Roy Rogers, Tony Curtis, Alan Ladd, and Natalie Wood all acted in movie scenes there. And it wasn't just Westerns: These hills can be seen in *Gladiator*, *Star Trek Generations*, *Iron Man*, *Django Unchained*, and the science fiction cult classic *Tremors*, among other productions. *Author photos*

END DETOUR

The train doesn't stop here anymore: The dilapidated Keeler railroad depot sits by a marker that reads "Keeler: End of the Line." The tracks of the Carson & Colorado narrow-gauge railroad from Mound House, east of Carson City, reached this point in 1883 and were supposed to go on to Mojave. But plans to extend them farther were abandoned when the nearby Cerro Gordo silver mine stopped turning a profit. *Author photos*

Finding Keeler

Location: About 15 miles southeast of Lone Pine via State Route 136 or 20 miles northeast of Olancha via SR 190 on the eastern side of Owens Lake

Above: An auto body shop sits next to the old Keeler Market.

Left: An abandoned gas station at the entrance to Keeler, just off State Route 136. *Author photos*

A single concrete wall, with a faded ad for A.B.C. Beer on the other side, is all that remains of this building in Keeler, where just 71 people still lived as of the 2020 census. *Author photos*

An abandoned
swimming pool,
center, and other
remnants of the
Keeler Beach and
Swim Club, built
around 1928.
Author photos

Owens Valley, with the mostly dry Owens Lake bed, looking from the northeast.
Dicklyon, CC BY-SA 4.0

Owens Lake

Owens Lake is a shadow of its former self. As the lake dried up—or, rather, was dried up via an aqueduct funneling its water to the Los Angeles basin—communities along its shores withered and died. What's left today are a few highway stops huddled close together on the western shore: Cartago, Olancha, and Grant, each with a population of 200 or fewer.

The dried-up lake is a product of a water war between the L.A. developers and the Owens Valley farmers. There were more of the former, and they had deeper pockets, so guess who won? But the Owens Valley folks didn't go down without a fight. In 1924, they laid explosives along the canal that was draining their lifeblood from the valley, then set off blasts that left 100-foot-long cracks in the concrete.

That fall, they followed up their sabotage by seizing control of the aqueduct and throwing open the gates to let the water roar back into the Owens River.

Dynamite left by saboteurs along the aqueduct in Owens Valley in 1924. *Los Angeles Times/Wikimedia Commons*

The Inyo County sheriff and two deputies were no match for 150 angry farmers, who refused to yield when confronted. They only backed down when a local banker whose brother had helped lead opposition to the aqueduct intervened. But the truce was only temporary. Three years later, with Los Angeles still making off with the water they needed to sustain their crops, an armed group surprised guards who had been charged with protecting the aqueduct and blasted away a 300-foot section of the pipeline.

The L.A. interests decided it was time to play hardball and sent out mounted men, armed with machine guns, with orders to shoot anyone who tried to sabotage the aqueduct again. The ranchers responded with their own armed force, carrying sawed-off shotguns and rifles.

Los Angeles only prevailed after all the banks in Owens Valley were shut down and the doors padlocked. It seemed the banker who had brokered the earlier cease-fire had been charged with cooking the books, embezzling nearly $900,000. He and his brother, who had supported the ranchers, were ultimately convicted, and the issue was decided.

A water tank along 395 beside what's left of Owens Lake touts the corridor as the "Gateway to the Eastern Sierra." *Author photo*

L.A. continued to pump water out of the Owens Valley to water lawns, golf courses, and parks in Southern California, and the ranches continued to dry up until they were abandoned. All that was left then were a few holdouts and some newcomers who decided to open businesses catering to travelers along the north-south highway that would soon become 395.

In a way, the ranchers got in the last, morbid laugh: The dam built to hold much of that water burst in 1928, sending a massive wall of water cascading all the way from the western Sierra to the Pacific Ocean, more than 50 miles away. More than 400 people were killed in the disaster.

But when L.A. continued to grow, the water-seekers returned in the mid-1930s with a new aqueduct and a new target: Mono Lake.

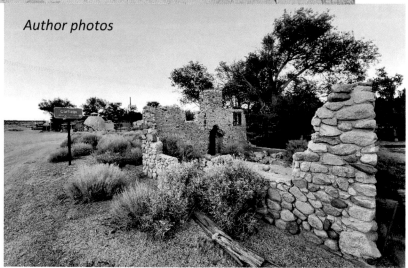

Author photos

The Cottonwood Creek kilns (top) on the western shore of Owens Lake produced charcoal during the 1870s that was ferried across to Keeler on one of two steamers for use in the ore smelters of Cerro Gordo. The two beehive kilns used wood from the Sierra Nevada to produce the charcoal because little wood was available on the eastern side of the lake. The remains of the kilns are visible today and are accessible via an unpaved road a couple of miles east of 395 and seven miles north of Cartago, named for the famed North African city of Carthage. Silver ingots from Cerro Gordo were ferried back across to the Cartago boat landing, near the ruins above on 395. The steamers cut a three-day trip around the lake down to three hours, but the enterprise ended when the larger of the two, the Bessie Brady, burned in 1882.

Finding Cartago

Location: About 20 miles south of Lone Pine on U.S. 395 and just 3 miles north of Olancha; Grant is just 2 miles farther south on the highway.

The California Alkali Co. opened this soda ash plant at Cartago in 1917 and operated it until 1932, harvesting alkaline deposits from the lake bed. Soda ash can be used to produce detergents, soaps, cosmetics and other material, especially glass.
Author photos

Central California had its Giant Orange stands, offering refreshment in the form of orange juice to overheated travelers before most cars had air conditioning. They've all vanished today, but Cartago still has a citrus-shaped roadside treat, even if it doesn't serve lemonade. The Lemon House Inn is of more recent vintage, although it didn't start out as a lemon at all. When it was constructed in 2006, it was just a plain white fiberglass dome. The owner, Vernon Lawson, installed metal cacti and a dinosaur sculpture three years later, then covered the structure itself in spray foam, carved out some windows and painted the whole thing "Ginster Yellow," the same color as his 1997 VW. In 2021, Lawson sold it to Vernon Alvarez, who turned it into the centerpiece for a motel along Highway 395. *Author photos*

Monstrous metallic entities populate the Olancha Sculpture Garden on the west side of 395. Artist Jael Hoffmann, a native of Israel who lived in Berlin before moving to the United States, created the sculptures, which stand up to 15 feet tall. Admission to the sculpture garden is free, and you can drive through. *Author photos*

A vacation guide ad, above, shows the Olancha Auto Service Garage and Texaco Service Station in 1954. The two photos top and center show the same buildings today. A café once occupied the larger garage building. The smaller canopied station was transformed into Gus' Fresh Jerky, which has been operating there since 1996. According to its website, Quentin Tarantino, Colin Farrell, and the Jonas Brothers have stopped by, and The Band Perry shot a music video there. *Author photos*

The sign above on State Route 190 near the 395 junction at Olancha points the way toward the Ranch House Café in Cartago, which is supposedly open from 7 a.m. to 8 p.m. for breakfast, lunch and dinner. The photo at top, however, tells a different story. *Author photos*

Finding Olancha

Location: 3 miles south of Cartago; 2 miles north of Grant

Route: U.S. 395/former U.S. 6

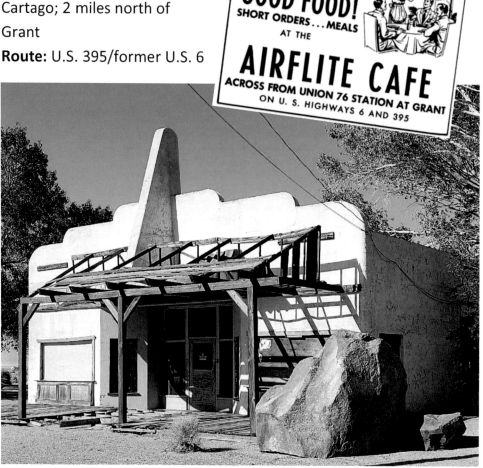

Frank & Ann's Airflite Café in Grant, seen in this 1957 ad and 2022 photo, was featured in the 1961 *Twilight Zone* episode "A Hundred Yards Over the Rim." In the episode, which aired during the show's second season, an 1847 wagon train pioneer winds up at a modern-day diner when he goes seeking help for his ill son. The episode featured familiar TV stars Cliff Robertson, John Astin of *The Addams Family*, and Ed Platt (the Chief from *Get Smart*). The wagon train scenes were filmed in the Olancha Dunes, and the next week's episode, "Rip Van Winkle Caper," was filmed up the road in the Alabama Hills. The café itself—called Joe's Airflite Café in the episode and sometimes spelled "Airflight" in real life—likely got its name from an airstrip behind the nearby Ranch Motel & Cabins. *Author photo*

Like the Airflite Café, Bill Wright's Union Oil Service Station across the highway is closed these days. The ad at right is from a 1957 vacation guide.

Author photos

STOP!
AT THE BIG 76 SIGN
AT GRANT
(1 MI. SO. OLANCHA)

MINUTE MAN SERVICE

FREE INFORMATION
ABOUT
Fishing - Hunting - Camping
CAMPFIRE PERMITS ISSUED
Clean Rest Rooms
Plenty of Parking Space
TRAILERS WELCOME!
BILL WRIGHT'S . . .
Union Oil Service Station
ON HIGHWAYS 395 & 6 . . . AT GRANT

The Rustic Oasis Motel in Olancha is described on Priceline as a "family-friendly motel" that "features a horseshoe pit and a fire pit for guest enjoyment." The roadside sign, however, had seen better days when this picture was taken in 2022.

The J.G. Motel in Grant later became the Ranch Motel & Cabins, site of the airstrip that likely gave the Airflite Café its name. Rooms with Beautyrest mattresses were $2.50 and up in 1948. A 1953 ad in the Los Angeles Times suggested that duck hunters "take your wife & camera north on Hiway 6 on road to Bishop to J.G. Motel at Grant, 180 miles from Los Angeles. Mgr. Mr. Thompson will give you free tour of 1000 acre duck club. Mallards now arriving. If interested in fishing, deer & bear hunting, ask to meet Ed Roman." The gabled motel is seen in 2023, above.

Author photo

Dunmovin

Dunmovin, 12 miles south of Grant, was founded in the early 20th century by James Cowan, who called it Cowan Station, moving it to the future U.S. 395 when the Midland Trail brought auto traffic through. The service station, store, and café closed in 1932 but was reopened four years later by Charles and Hilda King, who declared they were "done movin'." It stayed open until sometime in the 1970s.

Author photos

Little Lake

Much like Dunmovin, Little Lake served as a rest stop for motorists on a particularly lonely and isolated stretch of U.S. 395 at the edge of the Mojave Desert. The settlement is named for Owens Little Lake, which was dammed by the Los Angeles Department of Water and Power as it drained water from the once-fertile valley. Little Lake had a post office by 1909, and a single-story wooden hotel dating to the 1910s was replaced by the stone-front hotel in the photo in 1923; the café seems to have been added later. New owners took over in 1954, adding a swimming pool, souvenir shop and neon sign. But a later realignment of 395 left the hotel on a frontage road, and the narrow-gauge railroad that had served the community was removed in 1981. Business began to suffer in the 1960s, when cars could travel farther on a tank of gas. The hotel was converted into apartments, then it burned down in 1989. The post office closed seven years later, the offramps were removed, and nothing remains today of the roadside stop, seen here c. the 1940s. *Author collection*

Finding Little Lake (site)

Location: 12 miles south of Dunmovin; 17 miles north of U.S. 395-State Route 14 junction

Route: U.S. 395 and former U.S. 6

Pearsonville

The Golden Cactus Ghost Town Museum just north of Pearsonville on the west side of 395 is one of several "faux ghost town" roadside attractions in the area. There's one just south of Bishop called Brown's Town Campground and Country Store, and another a few miles south on SR 14 called Robber's Roost. It was closed as of this writing. *Author photos*

Finding Pearsonville

Location: 9 miles south of Little Lake and 57 miles south of Lone Pine; 8 miles north of U.S. 395-State Route 14 junction

Route: U.S. 395 and former U.S. 6

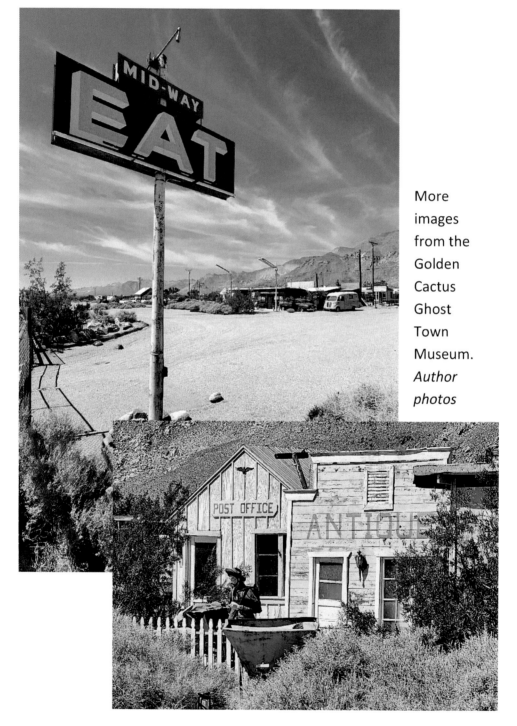

More images from the Golden Cactus Ghost Town Museum. *Author photos*

Pearsonville, a mile or so down from the Golden Cactus on the east side of the road, is pretty much a ghost town itself. The old business district, which includes the Trading Post (above) and mini mart/garage (below) is all fenced off and inaccessible to the public. The only thing open in town as of 2023 was a Shell station and convenience store on the corner. The population as of 2010 was listed at just 17, down from 27 in 2000. *Author photos*

Left: Pearsonville is presided over by this fiberglass "Uniroyal Gal," the female counterpart to the Muffler Men seen at roadside stops across the country. Muffler Men can be found in spacesuits, holding golf clubs, and in a variety of other guises, all based on the same mold created in the 1960s. Other Uniroyal Gals can be found in Hayward; Blackfoot, Idaho; Peoria, Illinois; Virginia, and New Jersey.

Below: Pearsonville is the self-proclaimed "Hub Cap Capital of the World" because resident Lucy Pearson is said to have 80,000 of them in her collection. *Author photos*

Inyokern

Inyokern, with barely 1,000 people, calls itself the "Sunshine Capital of America" and stands near the junction where U.S. 395 and U.S. 6 (now State Route 14) parted ways heading south at Bradys. The town, founded in 1909, was originally known simply as Siding 16, a reference to its railroad siding. The siding is still visible along the side of the main road. As its name suggests, it's in Kern County, just south of the Inyo County line. *Author photos*

Finding Inyokern

Location: 14 miles south of Pearsonville; 26 miles north of Red Mountain U.S. 395-State Route 14 junction

Route: State Route 178 (Inyokern Road) between U.S. 395 and SR 14

The view heading south toward San Bernardinoon old U.S. 395 and Route 66 near the Cajon Pass. *Author photo*

Epilogue: Southern California

Inyokern to San Diego   225 miles

Finding U.S. 395 in Southern California can be a bit of a challenge because it doesn't exist south of the place where it merges with modern Interstate 15 just north of San Bernardino.

Except that's not quite true.

U.S. 395 may not exist as a highway, but in many places, the road itself is still there. Or, more accurately, "roads." They just don't bear the 395 signs anymore, although some are still marked by brown rectangular signs that show you you're traveling on "historic" U.S. 395.

In many places, the highway has been supplanted by Interstates 215 and 15. In others, sections of old 395 are now maintained by the state of California, which has changed the numbers to fit its own system. Stretches of road that were once mapped as 395 are now State Route 74 between Perris and Lake Elsinore and SR 163 through San Diego.

The Southern California section of 395 is presented as an epilogue for this reason—and also because the region has become so built up (and out) that much of the old highway's character has been lost. It's been swallowed up by suburbs and strip malls that have replaced old landmarks and forever changed the once-rural character of the old road.

More than half a century has passed since U.S. 395 was decommissioned, a far longer span of time than it existed: from 1935 to 1969. Still, there are places you can find remnants of that bygone era if you know where to look.

Some of those remnants will be covered here.

Sierra Highway to Los Angeles

The old Sierra Highway veers away from U.S. 395 and heads southwest at Bradys (just west of Inyokern) as State Route 14. Once upon a time, this segment of road was part of U.S. 6, which shared the road with 395 from Bishop south to Inyokern before branching off westward. But that all ended when it was it was decommissioned beyond Bishop in 1964.

This westward route takes motorists through Mojave, Lancaster, and the Saugus area to a multi-layered I-5 interchange at the northern edge of the San Fernando Valley. This maze of concrete replaced a far simpler intersection with San Fernando Road (aka old U.S. 99).

SR 14, still signed as the Sierra Highway in Los Angeles County, roughly paralleled the Los Angeles Aqueduct. That massive project, completed in 1913, diverted water from the Owens River away from its natural flow to the Owens Lake just north of Independence to the booming San Fernando Valley.

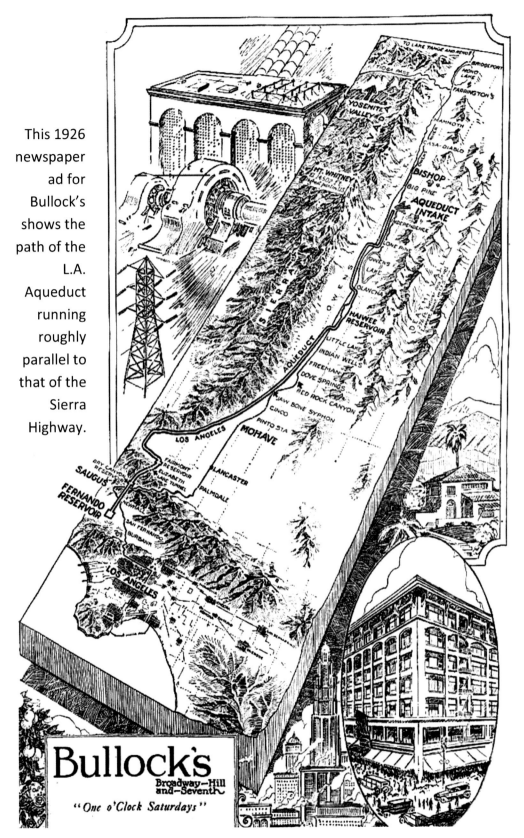

This 1926 newspaper ad for Bullock's shows the path of the L.A. Aqueduct running roughly parallel to that of the Sierra Highway.

The project, which ran through the red rock of Jawbone Canyon, destroyed agriculture in the Owens Lake basin while creating a suburban oasis just north of Los Angeles. Unfortunately, the St. Francis Dam, completed in 1926 to hold all that water, was so poorly designed and situated that it burst two years later, sending a wall of water crashing through all the way to the Pacific Ocean and killing hundreds.

Even that disaster, however, didn't keep Los Angeles from raiding the Owens Valley's water, which was needed to keep faucets flowing, lawns watered, and golf courses green in a newly flourishing suburbia.

The L.A. Aqueduct at the Owens River in 1913, below, and the pipeline to Los Angeles, left. *University of Southern California Libraries and California Historical Society*

SIERRA HIGHWAY

From top: Bradys Mobil, Red Rocks in Jawbone Canyon, and the Jawbone Canyon store. *Author photos*

Top: A team of horses lines up in front of the newspaper office in Lancaster around 1900 along the future Sierra Highway. *University of Southern California Libraries and California Historical Society*

Above: The Sierra Highway through Lancaster in 1918. The highway went south through Mojave, Lancaster, and Palmdale before turning west toward Santa Clarita. *Wikimedia Commons*

Top: An abandoned gas station on the Sierra Highway near Newhall.

Above: State Route 14 interchange with Interstate 5 near Santa Clarita.

Author photos

Top: TraveLodge on the Sierra Highway offered air-conditioned rooms and a swimming pool (musts in Mojave) on the Sierra Highway. The building was still there in 2023. *Author collection*

Above: The Budget Inn on SR 14 in Mojave, 2023. *Author photo*

395 to San Diego

While the Sierra Highway veers southwest, 395 heads southeast toward Inyokern, then south through miles of desert toward San Bernardino. There isn't much along this section of highway, but there's plenty of history—and a little frustration in the form of some heavy traffic and a 15-mile straightaway where you can't pass.

It's not just that you shouldn't. You can't. Yes, there are "Do Not Pass" signs on the side of the road, but they're hardly necessary. In fact, they're almost comical because permanent cones in the center of the highway provide an effective deterrent against any attempt to get around that slow-poke big-rig in front of you.

But your patience will be rewarded: You'll run into a couple of ghost towns, a section of abandoned highway, and a major intersection called Kramer Junction where you'll have a chance to stock up on necessities for the ride ahead or get a bite to eat.

It's south of Kramer Junction that you'll hit the no-passing zone, and not much farther on (past Adelanto as you head toward San Bernardino), U.S. 395 disappears from the map.

This is where the highway joined Route 66, one of several highways that shared the same road with 395 in Southern California before they were replaced by state highways and interstates—specifically 215 and 15—in the late 1960s and early '70s. In addition to the "mother road," 395 shared the roadway with U.S. 91 between San Bernardino and Riverside, and then with U.S. 60 for a brief stretch.

It then headed south through towns like Perris, Elsinore (which changed its name to Lake Elsinore in 1972), and Temecula en route to San Diego. Here's a look at some of the streets 395 followed in Southern California, as we continue heading south.

San Bernardino — Cajon Boulevard (U.S. 66) into town
       Mt. Vernon Avenue south
       La Cadena southwest to Riverside*
Riverside — 1st Street west from La Cadena
       Main Street into town
       8th Street (now University) east at Main/Market
Perris — U.S. 60 cosigned into town
       4th Street west through town, curving onto State Route 74
       Southeast on 74 to Lake Elsinore
*Look for old concrete running parallel at Fogg Avenue in Colton

SIERRA HIGHWAY

Lake Elsinore — Collier Avenue south, paralleling modern I-15
      Main Street through town to Palomar Street southeast
      (Palomar becomes Washington Street south of town)
Temecula —Jefferson Avenue into town
      (Jefferson becomes Old Front Street downtown)

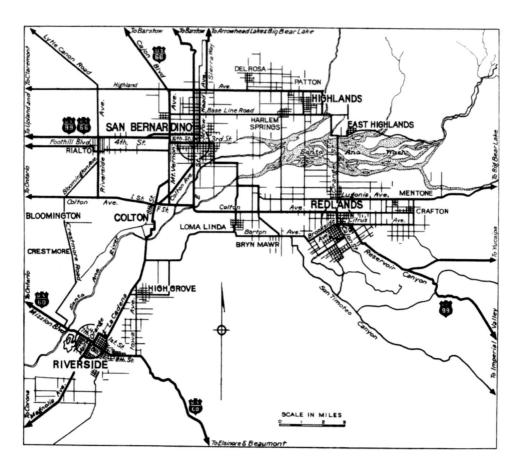

South of Temecula, 395 becomes two different roads: the original alignment, which carried the federal highway shield from 1935 until 1949, and the highway that replaced it, in use from 1949 until it was, in turn, decertified and supplanted by the interstate system in 1969.

That was more than half a century ago, but you can still follow either one of those alignments today, and you can be sure you're on the right path if you see the Historic 395 markers along the way.

1935 alignment

Heading south from Temecula, the original alignment of U.S. 395 went on an out-of-the-way western loop through Fallbrook and Bonsall on Mission Road. Vista and San Marcos, both cities of about 100,000 people today, were little more than roadside stops when 395 passed through: Each had fewer than 2,000 residents, and neither would be incorporated until 1963.

The next big city along this route was Escondido, which motorists traveling south would enter from the west via Mission (now State Route 78). The new, more direct route, by contrast, followed the course of future Interstate 15 and entered Escondido from the north, continuing through town on Centre City Parkway, which is now signed as I-15 Business.

South of Escondido, the two alignments went their separate ways again near Lake Hodges. The 1935 highway headed down Pomerado Road through Poway, a stretch of road that includes a couple of interesting features. A brief detour to the west at the Pomerado exit from I-15 will take you to the site of the old Lake Hodges Bridge, built in 1919 and later incorporated into 395.

Then, as you travel south on Pomerado past Scripps Poway Parkway, you can find a short segment of abandoned roadway just east of Pomerado at Stonemill Drive, extending about halfway to Legacy Road. (You have to climb down a hill to see it.)

The original version of 395 continued south on Pomerado Road back to I-15, where it becomes Miramar Road. At that point, old 395 turned south again on Kearny Villa Road and on through Murphy Canyon to Camino Del Rio (paralleling modern I-8 and the San Diego River), where it jogged briefly eastward before heading south again and entering San Diego on Fairmount Avenue.

From there, it turned west on El Cajon Boulevard (U.S. 80), then south on Park Boulevard into Balboa Park, home of numerous historical buildings dating to 1915 as well as to the San Diego Zoo.

Future U.S. 395 at Miramar Road north of San Diego, c. 1920s.

Author collection

1949 alignment

The newer 1949 alignment, meanwhile followed the course later chosen for I-15, skirting Poway to the west. Another old bridge is visible in this area: the 1949 Penasquitos Creek arch bridge, which now stands alongside a newer bridge that carries Interstate 15. These days, the old arch bridge—itself an improvement over the previous 1920 road, which ran along a hillside—is open to pedestrians and cyclists only. You can access it by taking the Scripps Poway Parkway exit east and turning immediately back north on Cara Way, which parallels I-15.

Instead of following the modern I-15 corridor all the way into San Diego, however, the newer version of 395 paralleled modern State Route 163 on Linda Vista Road, forking left from Linda Vista at the city limits and heading directly south to Balboa Park and the San Diego Zoo.

The following pages contain some photos and information to help you navigate the history of old U.S. 395 in Southern California.

Randsburg

Randsburg is actually a mile and a half west of 395, half an hour south of the 14/395 split. It's one of the most complete ghost towns you'll find along the way and well worth the brief detour. The town sprang up after gold was discovered in the area in 1895. Two years later, it boasted 300 buildings and a population of about 2,500, and construction began on its first stamp mill in 1898. A fire burned down half the town that same year, but there's still plenty to see, including historic buildings on Butte Avenue (the main street through town), old mine equipment and the historic city jail. The General Store, above, dates to 1903. *Author photos*

The Randsburg City Jail's only inhabitant these days, right. The town's mines churned out more than $60 million in gold profits between 1895 and 1933. Movies like *Hidalgo* and *Cowboys and Aliens* have been filmed in Randsburg, where you can find the White House Saloon, Randsburg Inn, a museum, and other vintage buildings. *Author photos*

Johannesburg, founded to support mining operations in nearby Randsburg, and Red Mountain (pictured above) sit about a mile apart on 395—known as Broadway Avenue in Jo-Burg. *Author photos*

Most gas stations and garages in the area have closed up shop, but there was still an open Texaco station at the south end of Johannesburg in 2023.

The Silver Dollar Saloon and Owl Café are two historic watering holes on the highway in Red Mountain (originally known as Osdick). Both were speakeasies during Prohibition, when actor Fatty Arbuckle was known to visit and sneak a drink, and among 30 saloons that once lined the road here.

Top: The Silver Dollar opened as The Northern in 1919 to serve miners drawn to the area by the discovery of silver at the Kelly Mine—the richest silver mine in the country at the time, producing some $13 million worth of ore.

Above: Slim Riffle founded the Owl Café around 1921 and added the Owl Hotel nearby the following year. The original building burned down in 1929, and Riffle replaced it with a wooden building he hauled in from Atolia, just to the south. Over the years, Orson Welles, Rita Hayworth, and others visited. But first and foremost, The Owl was a place for miners to drink, gamble, fight, and find female companionship. There was even a call box with eight brass fittings for house prostitutes, who entertained customers in their "cribs" out back. Today, it's a mining museum and shop. *Author photos*

Kramer Junction

RESTAURANT

Nearly an hour south of the 14/395 split, you'll come to Kramer Junction, otherwise known as Four Corners. Until 2020, you probably felt cornered when you arrived there. That's when work was finally completed on an expressway bypass for State Route 58, which crosses 395 here to create the aforementioned "four corners." SR 58 runs from Barstow in the east through Mojave and Bakersfield, then on to the California coast, serving as a major artery for truckers (which constitute half the average daily traffic) transporting goods to the San Joaquin Valley. *Author photos*

On the highway, 2020

"On Thursday, the agency [Caltrans] opened a nine-mile stretch that allows motorists crossing the Mojave Desert to bypass a stoplight at a critical intersection of Highway 58 and U.S. Route 395. ... An average of 14,100 tractor-trailers per day crossed the west side of that intersection in 2016, according to Caltrans records. Some say the resulting delays along Highway 58, which has only two lanes in that area, were known to last as long as half an hour."

— *Bakersfield.com, October 29*

These signs were all that remained in 2023 of Astro Burger, which opened in 1972 and drew the inspiration for its name from the Space Shuttle program at nearby Edwards Air Force Base (its main competitor was called the Shuttle). Astro Burger served more than a dozen burgers, including the top-of-the-line Colossal Burger, along with sandwiches and shakes. It closed in 2020.

Mascot cartoon, author photos

An abandoned section of U.S. 395 crosses a hill just west of the current highway a mile or two south of Kramer Junction. *Author photo*

Adelanto

If you like marble statues and meditation, the Vien Chan Nguyen Buddhist temple is just off 395 in Adelanto. The center features dozens of marble statues ranging from lions to dragons, and a 24-foot-tall statue of Buddhist saint Quan yin. It has grown quickly since its founding around 2008, much like Adelanto itself, which has a population of 38,000 in 2020, up from just over 8,500 in 1990. *Author photos*

DETOUR ▸ Victorville

Top: The western edge of Victorville is on 395, but you'll need to take a short detour east to see a few interesting attractions on Route 66, which shares the road with 395 a bit farther to the south. Among them is the California Route 66 museum, which opened in 1995 and features more than 4,500 feet of floor space packed with memorabilia and interactive photo-op exhibits like a re-created '50s diner and an old Model T. It's open Thursdays through Sundays at 16825 D Street (Route 66, naturally).

Above: The New Corral Motel, with a neon sign from 1947, is one of a few Route 66 relics left in town. *Author photos*

SIERRA HIGHWAY

Left: Water tower just east of the 395/66 junction.

Below: This Victorville Route 66 café opened in 1947 and became Emma Jean's Holland Burger in 1979, named for the wife of new owner Richard Gentry. It was featured in Quentin Tarantino's 2004 film *Kill Bill: Volume 2. Author photos*

Left: The Green Spot Motel is a survivor from 1937, when it opened on Route 66 in Victorville as a 21-unit U-shaped motor court. A Green Spot Café across the road burned down in 1954. *Author photo*

END DETOUR

The Outpost Café sits at the current southern end of U.S. 395, where it once merged with Route 66 and now feeds onto Interstate 15. The Outpost began as a six-seat diner and gas stop (Douglas gasoline, with the winged-heart logo) in 1929, moving across the road in 1961 to make room for the construction of I-15. Menu items such as chicken salad, meatloaf, chicken fried steak, and burgers cater to truckers who love the place. *Author photos*

Cajon Pass

OUTPOST CAFE

8685 HWY. 395

From top:
Original picnic table, "C" marker, and reconstructed stone monument that stood on the site (together with an Auto Club road marker).
Author photos

The Santa Fe Railroad donated land for a welcome station to serve motorists crossing Cajon Pass on the National Old Trails Highway in 1919. Only later would the roadway between the San Bernardino and San Gabriel mountains become U.S. 395 and Route 66. The Elks Club built a stone lodge, and the site included a store, post office, cooking stoves, barbecue pits, and more. Unfortunately, it was all destroyed in a devastating flood in 1938.

On the highway, 1919

Site of Camp Cajon.
Author photo

"Directly beside the boulevard through Cajon Pass and at an elevation of 3000 feet, Camp Cajon furnishes an unusually delightful situation for a motor camp ground... Twenty-four concrete tables with concrete seats around them, accommodating eight persons, provide for the convenience of visitors at meal times... A well, with an old-fashioned pump, provides that vital necessity of a good camp ground, an abundance of pure water. It is the intention, as soon as funds are available, to build a series of stone fireplaces along the eastern border of the camp for the further convenience of the tourist."

— *Los Angeles Times, July 27*

Left: If you look carefully, you'll see an old "EAT" sign in the trees west of the road. One place to eat for many years was the Summit Inn, which was built in 1952 but burned down in 2016. Another was Meekers Café, with its gas station, motel, and grocery store, where Camp Cajon campers a quarter-mile south took refuge in the 1938 flood. Ezra Meeker ran the place from 1918 until his death in 1966. *Author photos*

Above: A 1930 bridge on the old U.S. 66/395 alignment.

A 1930s-era stone guard rail lines the Cajon Pass road in some places. The highway through Cajon Pass was the successor to Brown's Turnpike, a toll road built in the 1860s. Its owners charged a quarter for a man on horseback and $1 for a wagon to use the road. In the early 1900s, the National Old Trails Road followed the Santa Fe rail line down an 18 percent grade into Blue Cut Canyon and on to Devore, which had a store where you could stock up on supplies. If you needed to stop before that, you could do so seven miles earlier at the Cosy (or Cozy) Dell Store. *Author photo*

On the highway, 1915

"Following the railroad more or less closely, a newly constructed highway leads from Needles 170 miles along the Mojave Desert to Barstow, where a turn to the south is made and the descent begins along a splendid road through Cajon Pass to San Bernardino. The desert is past and the fruit orchards stretch in every direction. From San Bernardino, the run is made via Riverside to the San Diego exposition."

— ***The Automobile Journal, February 10***

San Bernardino

The Lido Motel sits in the shadow of a modern overpass on Mt. Vernon Avenue, former U.S. 395, entering San Bernardino from the north. Route 66 followed the same path, although a business route known as "City 66" diverged from the Cajon highway southeast into the city on Kendall Drive, then headed south on E Street, site of the first McDonald's restaurant (below). The McDonald brothers, Mac and Richard, opened the first "Golden Arches" at 1398 North E Street at West 14th in 1948. Today, it's a museum. *Author photos*

Route 66 leaves old 395 and turns west from Mt. Vernon onto 5th Avenue, which becomes Rialto Avenue and, farther on, Foothill Boulevard. The Wigwam Motel is just a couple of miles west of Mt. Vernon on Rialto and well worth a detour. It's one of seven built in the South and Southwest during the 1930s and '40s, three of which remain: No. 7 in San Bernardino; No. 6 In Holbrook, Arizona (also on Route 66); and No. 2 in Cave City, Kentucky. *Author photos*

Colton

You'll find this abandoned section of old 395 concrete just east of La Cadena Drive (old 395) off Fogg Avenue in Colton. From Fogg, turn right before the railroad underpass at top left, just after the fire station. The concrete is a block down, beside a park. *Author photos*

Riverside

The Fox Riverside Theatre opened in June of 1929 with 1,550 seats, including a balcony level. The theater, on the northwest corner of Market Street and Mission Inn Avenue (formerly 7th Street) hosted Vivian Leigh for a sneak preview of *Gone With the Wind* in 1939. Today, it's a performing arts center. *Author photos*

Views of the Mission Inn in 2023 author photos and (at bottom) in 1915 during the Pasear, courtesy of McCurry Foto. The inn began as an adobe boarding house called The Glenwood Cottage in 1876 and became the Glenwood Mission Inn under owner Frank Miller in 1902. It now occupies a city block.

Glenwood Garage, seen here during the Pasear, stood just across Main Street from the Mission Inn on 7th Street (now Mission Inn Avenue). The garage was open as early as 1909 on an important thoroughfare through town. U.S. 395 ultimately ran a block south of the inn and garage on 8th Street (now University Avenue) before heading out of town on Box Springs Road. From the north, it entered Riverside on La Cadena, jogged west on 1st Street to Main, then moved a block farther west to Market before veering back east on 8th. *McCurry Foto*

On the highway, 1909

"Riverside's first automobile show opened today in the Glenwood Garage on Seventh Street, with all the latest tourist cars on exhibition. ... The unique mission garage is gaily decorated with large flags of all nations, from the private collection of Frank Miller, flowers, palms and a string of electric lights. The show is conducted under the auspices of Frank A. Miller of the Glenwood; Ed E. Miller, manager of the Glenwood Garage... and others."

— *Los Angeles Times, February 6*

1935 alignment

Riverside to San Diego

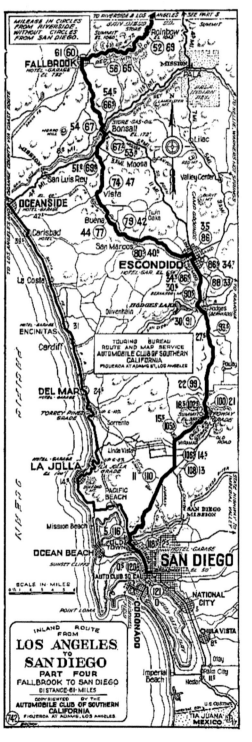

Perris

U.S. 395 shared the road with U.S. 60 briefly east of Riverside, curving gradually south to Perris. The desert town had barely 1,000 residents when 395 was first signed in California but counted nearly 80,000 in 2020. *Author photos*

The 568-seat Art Deco Perris Theatre (top) opened two blocks north of the highway on D Street in 1946. The Southern Hotel, just south of the highway on D Street, dates back to 1886 and is the oldest commercial building still standing in town.

Lake Elsinore

The 1924 Methodist Church, above, and the 1887 Armory on Main Street, right, both predated the street's identity as a portion of U.S. 395—and have outlasted it, as well. Only historical markers such as the one above remain. Lake Elsinore was known as just Elsinore until 1972, when residents voted to change the name. The population surpassed 3,000 for the first time in 1970, and a half-century later, more than 70,000 people live there. (The church is now a cultural center.) *Author photos*

The 1st National Bank of Temecula had the roadside virtually all to itself when it was built in 1914. Now, old 395 is lined with buildings through town. The first concrete structure in town, it served as a bank until 1943 and eighty years later housed a Mexican restaurant.
Photos by author, right, and Sharon Marie Provost, below

Temecula

The 10-room Palomar Hotel started out in 1927 as the Hotel McCulloch, named for owner Lena McCulloch. It became the Palomar a decade later, and at one time included a soda fountain, drugstore, and later, a post office. It's supposedly haunted, with some guests even claiming to have heard screeching noises outside and felt the Native American bird totem over the front entrance poke them on the shoulder with its beak, leaving black and white feathers behind.

Right: The Rainbow Oaks Restaurant, founded in 1946 and renovated by new owners around 2009, still sports this vintage neon sign (with ad below for RC Cola). Yes, the neon still lights up at night.

Below: Postmile marker for old 395 in San Diego County, showing number of miles to San Diego.

Above: The Mission Theatre was built in 1936 on Main Street, part of the first U.S. 395 alignment in Fallbrook. *Author photos*

Escondido

Top: The Sunkist packing house was built in 1934 along Mission Avenue at the western entrance to town, a year before it was signed as the first 395 alignment. Torn down to make way for a post office, it once served 500-plus local growers and, when built, was said to have the widest Arch-Rib trussless roof ever installed. *Library of Congress*

Above: Eucalyptus trees were often planted along U.S. highways such as 99 and 101 in California, and they still line this stretch of old 395 in Escondido called Centre City Parkway/Business 15. *Author photo*

These two images show the old Lake Hodges Bridge about 5 miles south of Escondido, which was built for $80,000 in 1919—a year after the Lake Hodges Dam was built, creating the reservoir. Originally called Bernardo Station Bridge, the concrete H-frame structure carried U.S. 395 until it was demolished in 1968. *Photos courtesy of Joel Windmiller*

Poway

This abandoned section of old 395 is just down the hill from Pomerado Road—another old alignment—in Poway. Weeds and bushes have cracked the asphalt, and a wooden structure has been plopped down on the old roadway.

The abandoned road is just east of Pomerado and south of Stonemill Drive. Note the eucalyptus trees in the image at left. *Author photos*

Take Scripps Poway Parkway west from Pomerado Road to the new alignment next to I-15, then head north on a vestige of 1949-era 395, now called Cara Way (left). At the end, you'll find the arch bridge at top right, paralleling the newer I-15 bridge. The new bridge was first built in 1966, and the arch bridge is now used only by cyclists and pedestrians. *Author photos*

San Diego

Photos from the 1912 Pasear Tour show a mountain road in San Diego County and the San Diego Mission. *McCurry Foto*

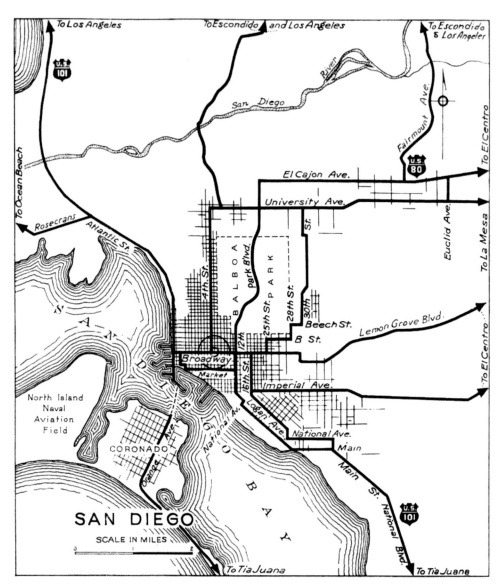

This 1930s map shows the original path of U.S. 395 entering San Diego from the north via Fairmount Avenue to El Cajon Avenue (then U.S. 80), then heading west before traveling south again into Balboa Park.

Balboa Park was a natural destination for U.S. 395. San Diego's centerpiece even today, it was the site of the Panama California Exposition in 1915. Buildings constructed for that celebration still draw tourists more than a century later. The promotional photo for the expo at top shows the road snaking under the Cabrillo Bridge then, and the photo directly above (courtesy of Joel Windmiller) shows the road sometime around the 1940s. The photos on the following page show the park and highway today.

Top photo 2023 by author; center photo 2019 by Alfred Twu via Wikimedia Commons; bottom photo by Sharon Marie Provost

Top: Billboards along El Cajon Boulevard, former U.S. 80, which shared the highway with 395 heading into San Diego for several years.

Above: Rush-hour traffic in San Diego from that same year, 1941. *Photos by Russell Lee, Farm Security Administration.*

Sources

"1st National Bank of Temecula," temeculaca.gov.

"102nd Annual Genoa Candy Dance," visitcarsonvalley.org.

"About the Bodie Hotel," thebodiehotel.com.

"About Ravendale, CA," places.us.com.

"About Us: Modoc National Wildlife Refuge," fws.gov.

Akeman, Thom. "Quakes Near Mammoth Lakes Shake Much Of State," Sacramento Bee, p. 1, May 26, 1980.

"Alabama Hills Brochure," blm.gov.

"Alabama Hills Natural Arch," sierranevadageotourism.org.

"Ancil 'Bruce' Morse" (obituary), Santa Cruz Sentinel, p. 8, Nov. 9, 1995.

"Andruss Motel," monocounty.org.

"Andruss Motel," roadsidepeek.com.

"The Automobile Journal," Vol. XXXIX, No. 1, Feb. 10, 1915.

"Back in 1893 Reno Had a Champion Team," Nevada State Journal, p. S-1, July 29, 1945.

"Bank Saloon," National Register of Historic Places Nomination Form, npgallery.nps.gov.

Barber, Alicia. "Barnes Radio Service," renohistorical.org.

Barber, Alicia. "Club Cal-Neva," renohistorical.org.

Barber, Alicia. "Frolich Building," renohistorical.org.

Barber, Alicia. "Giraudo Building," renohistorical.org.

Barber, Alicia. "Sewell's Supermarket," renohistorical.org.

Barber, Alicia. "Woolworth's Building," renohistorical.org.

Barber, Phil and Moreno, Richard. "Monday example of how Slide Mountain got name," Reno Gazette-Journal, p. 3, May 31, 1983.

Bartell, John. "Sour accommodations: A night at Lemon House Inn," abc10.com, July 14, 2022.

"Best Hot Springs in Mammoth Lakes Area, California," luxuryunderbudget.com.

Bodine, Mike. "Merry Go Round," easternsierranevada.com, Dec. 25, 2017.

Bodine, Mike. "They only moved the headstones," thesheetnews.com, Oct. 30, 2015.

Branson-Pitts, Hailey. "A prostitute's ghost and bullet holes: In rural California hotels, spookiness is the appeal," losangelestimes.com, May 26, 2023.

Breckenridge, Karl. "Demise of the Grand Central, Overland hotels," rgj.com, July 12, 2014.

"C.C. Directors Delay Action on Name Change, Reno Evening Gazette, p. 3, April 1, 1952.

"Cajon Pass Auto Camp Destroyed," San Bernardino Daily Sun, p. 12, March 4, 1938.

"California State 203; the road that could have been a Trans-Sierra Highway," gribblenation.org, July 6, 2017.

"Camps for Motorists," Los Angeles Times, Part 6, p. 6, July 27, 1919.

Capps, Steven A. "How the West is run," San Francisco Examiner, July 9, 1989.

"Carson Street Construction," Scott Schrantz, aroundcarson.com, Oct. 10, 2020.

"Casa Diablo," noehill.com.

Catton, Theodore and Krahe, Diane L. "The Sands of Manzanar," National Park Service, oah.org, 2018.

"Celebrity Customers," freshjerky.com.

"Census of Population: Number of Inhabitants, California," www2.census.gov.

"Chimney Rock Historical Monument," sierrageotourism.org.

"Chimney Rock's Roadside Cousin Earthcache," geocaching.com.

"Citrus Fruit & Forests – the Story of California's Fruit Growers Supply Company," fruitgrowers.com.

"Comfort, Convenience & Fun," andrussmotel.com.

"Convict Lake," monocounty.org.

"'The Corner Store' (Formerly The Bank of Surprise Valley), Townsend and Main Streets, Cedarville surprisevalleychamber.com

Cox, John. "New segment of Highway 58 at Route 395 relieves bottleneck, opens way for Kern distribution Activity," bakersfield.com, Oct. 29, 2019.

"Cressler and Bonner Building, Main Street, Cedarville,"surprisevalleychamber.com.

"Cressler and Bonner Trading Post, 1865 (No. 14 California Historic Landmark)," sierranevadageotourism.org.

Cuoso, Jeremy. "Wheels West Day in Susanville History-April 20th, 1926," susanvillestuff.com, April 20, 2015.

Cuoso, Susan. "From the Files of the Lassen Historical Society: The Cindercone Ballroom," susanvillestuff.com, July 30, 2020.

Cuoso, Susan. "From the Files of the Lassen Historical Society: The Standish Colony," susanvillestuff.com, March 4, 2021.

Cuoso, Susan. "From the Files of the Lassen Historical Society: The Susanville Elk's Hall," susanvillestuff.com, May 21, 2020.

D.S. Denehy ads, 1901-1938, Alturas New Era.

Daugherty, William. "Alva Gould – Discoverer of the Famous Gould and Curry Mine," legendsofamerica.com.

"Davis Creek," Alturas Plaindealer, p. 1, Dec. 22, 1938.

"Davis Creek," Modoc County Record, p. 5, March 25, 1954.

"Davis Creek Community Church," noehill.com.

"Davis Creek News," Modoc County Record, p. 8, April 3, 1952.

"Dechambeau Hotel and I.O.O.F. Building," bodie.com.

"Deputy Slain By Indian at Bishop, Calif.," Santa Ana Register, p. 10, Jan. 23, 1925.

DeVeir, Eve. "Milford Country Store Opens," Lassen County Times, Local Business Review, May 20, 1997.

"The Devil's Garden," fs.usda.gov.

"Discover Minden: A Walking Tour," townofminden.com.

Do, Phi, Lu Jennifer, and Ylanan, Aida. "The 'No-Nos' of Tule Lake," latimes.com, March 20, 2021.

"Dunmovin," beyond.nvexpeditions.com.

"E. Lauer & Sons Ghost Sign - Alturas, CA," waymarking.com.

"Edward S. Hall," obituary, Santa Clarita Signal, p. 6, Sept. 23, 2012.

"El Camino Sierra is in Poor Shape," Oakland Tribune, p. 35, Sept. 13, 1914.

"A Fire At Night," Oakland Tribune, p. 5, April 14, 1888.

"Funeral of Euell Bussey Held Friday," Alturas Plaindealer, p. 5, June 27, 1934.

"Gaming History – Week of October 25, 2015," museumofgaminghistory.org.

"Genoa Bar & Saloon," travelnevada.com.

"Giant Women: The Uniroyal Gal," roadsideamerica.com.

Gill, Shayla. "Pair suspected in hotel murder will face trial," Lassen County Times, p. 1, May 2, 1995.

Glass, Gary B. "Proceedings of the First International Soda Ash Conference, Volume I," owensvalleyhistory.com, 1998.

Glionna, John. "Dealing with town's split personality," Modesto Bee, p. A-7, Aug. 15, 2005.

"Golden Hotel Is Dead at 56," Reno Evening Gazette, p. 11, April 3, 1962.

Gorman, Tom. "Landmark or Not, Building Seems Doomed," latimes.com, Aug. 9, 1989.

"A Great Circuit Highway," Berkeley Daily Gazette, p. 4, Dec. 19, 1911.

Harmon, Mella Rothwell. "Pioneer Center for the Performing Arts," renohistorical.org.

Harmon, Mella Rothwell. "Washoe County Courthouse," renohistorical.org.

"Harrah's makes plans for parking," Reno Evening Gazette, p. 17, June 8, 1977.

"Harrah's Reno Permanently Ceased Gaming Operation on March 17, 2020," caesars.com.

Henley, David C. "Was legendary Kit Carson ever in Churchill County?" nevadaappeal.com. Oct. 24, 2013.

Hillinger, Charles. "Sulo Lasko owns the whole town," Redding Record Searchlight, p. 5, Oct. 22, 1983.

"The History of the Carson City Mint," usmint.gov, August 5, 2015.

"History of the Dow Hotel and Dow Villa Motel," dowvillamotel.com.

"History of Gardnerville," townofgardnerville.com.

"History of Mormon Station State Historic Park," parks.nv.gov.

"History of the Museum," museumofwesternfilmhistory.org.

"Holiday in Bishop in Honor of the Tourists," San Francisco Chronicle, p. 13, June 19, 1912.

"Hotel California Now Open for Business," Alturas Plaindealer, p. 1, July 10, 1935.

Hunter, Shaun. "Cottonwood Creek Charcoal Kilns," outdoorproject.com.

Hunter, Shaun. "Olancha Sculpture Garden," outdoorproject.com.

"Improvements at Tioga Lodge," Gardnerville Record-Courier, p. 2, June 18,1920.

"J. Niles Would Approve Of Hotel Restoration," rootsweb.com.

"Jael Hoffman," jsculpt.com.

James, Rachel. "Notes From the Field: Abandoned Brothel of Secret Valley," atlasobscura.com, June 27, 2013.

"Jess Valley Schoolhouse," National Register of Historic Places Registration Form, npgallery.nps.gov.

"Jolly Kone," karaokejapas38.com.

"JT Basque History Is Broad & Rich," visitcarsonvalley.org.

"June Lake, Grant Lake, Rush Creek, Culver's Camp and surrounding areas," owensvalleyhistory.com.

"June Lake Loop: A scenic drive in the Eastern Sierra!" roadtrippingcalifornia.com.

"Kit Carson Trail," visitcarsoncity.com.

"Kittie Lee Inn at Bishop Ready For Big Year," Los Angeles Evening Express, p. 19, May 21, 1926.

"Lassen County Court House," National Register of Historic Places Registration Form, npgallery.nps.gov.

"Latest Models are Exhibited," Los Angeles Times, p. 21, Feb. 6, 1909.

"Lava Beds National Monument," nps.gov.

"Lemoyne Hazard," owensvalleyhistory.com.

Lindstrom, Natasha. "Buddhist Meditation Center grows in size influence in Adelanto," vvdailypress.com, Oct. 17, 2011.

"Little Waldorf Saloon Concert History," concerarchives.org.

"Long Valley Caldera Field Guide – Devil's Postpile," usgs.gov.

"Long Valley Caldera Field Guide – Mono Lake," usgs.gov.

"Long Valley Caldera Field Guide – Obsidian Dome," usgs.gov.

"Local Merchant Passes at Redding," Surprise Valley Record, June 1, 1932.

Lu, Lynn Q. "Truckers Say This Dusty Roadside Diner Is California's Best Restaurant," la.eater.com, Jan. 18, 2023.

"Mammoth Company History Timeline," zippia.com.

"Many Autos Are Coming," Gardnerville Record-Courier, p. 1, June 14, 1912.

"Manzanar: Historic Resource Study/Special History Study," nps.gov.

"Methodist Church," bodie.com.

"Minarets/Minaret Vista - Ansel Adams Wilderness," sierranevadageotourism.org.

"The Modoc County Library Building, Formerly the Bank of America Building, 460 Main Street," surprisevalleychamber.com.

"Modoc Has Real 'Chimney Rock'," Sacramento Bee, p. 16, Dec. 29, 1926.

"Modoc NF History, 1945 -- Chapter I, General Description," fsusda.gov.

"Modoc NF History, 1945 — Chapter II, Early History," fs.usda.gov.

"Modoc National Forest, Chapter VI Timber," fs.usda.gov.

Moreno, Richard. "The Nevada Traveler: Niles Hotel is the beating heart of Alturas, Calif.," nevadaappeal.com, Nov. 3, 2021.

Moreno, Richard. "On the trail of George Wingfield," nevadaappeal.com, Jan. 6, 2022.

"Motor Parties on Good Roads Tour," Bakersfield Morning Echo, p. 11, June 21, 1912.

"Move Post Office," Reno Evening Gazette, p. 12, Dec. 4, 1957.

Mullen, Frank X. "In 100 years, the Little Waldorf Saloon morphed from speakeasy to Reno icon," renonr.com, March 22, 2022.

"Neon Sign Is Placed On New Sierra Theatre," Lassen Mail, p. 1, Feb. 15, 1935.

"Nevada Club, the way Reno used to be," sonic.net.

"Nevada History," visitcarsoncity.com.

"Nevada Place Names Population 1860-2000," blackrockdesert.org.

"Nevada State Capitol," carson.org.

"New Bowling Alley Opening Set Here," Reno Evening Gazette, p. 13, Nov. 11, 1958.

"New Pine Creek," Klamath Falls Herald and News, p. 3, Aug. 14, 1948.

"New Pine Creek News," Alturas Plaindealer, p. 5, July 18, 1934.

Nolan, Michael. "Randsburg: Living ghost town is a Mojave Desert treasure," sbsun.com, July 24, 2016.

"Old Mammoth, the Meadow," The Album: Times & Tales of Inyo-Mono, Vol. V, No. 3, owensvalleyhistory.com, 1992.

"The Oldsmobile," Alturas New Era, p. 3, Oct. 11, 1918.

"Onion Valley Road; former California State Route 180 to Kearsarge Pass," gribblenation.org, Aug. 30, 2020.

"Ortiz Hung!" Reno Evening Gazette, p. 3, Sept. 19, 1891.

"Our Story," nileshotel.com.

"Our Story," walker-burger.com.

"Overland Restaurant & Pub," travelnevada.com.

"Owens Valley Cottonwood Charcoal Kilns Highway 395," daytrippen.com, Jan. 3, 1923.

"The Owl 'Café.' Red Mountain & The Kelly Silver Mine History," redmtnkellysilver.com.

"Packed Away," somewhereoutwest.us, Feb. 15, 2018.

"Palomar Hotel," vailranch.org.

"The Palomar Inn, Temecula," nightlyspirits.com.

"Pathfinding Trip By Automobilists," San Francisco Examiner, p. 8, June 9, 1912.

"Pauline Prole Obituary," legacy.com.

Perkins, Eloise. "Old Hodges bridge," North County Nuggets, Escondido Times-Advocate, p. 7,
          Jan. 25, 1968.

"Prepare for a Restless Night at Temecula's Very Haunted Palomar Inn," backpackerverse.com.

Purdy, Tim. "Lake Goes Dry," Exploring Lassen County's Past, tipurdy.org, Aug. 29, 2022.

Purdy, Tim. "A Ravendale School Story," Exploring Lassen County's Past, tipurdy.org, March 9, 2019.

Purdy, Tim. "Standish's Landmark Store," Exploring Lassen County's Past, tipurdy.org, Oct. 25, 2016.

Purdy, Tim. "Sunkist & The Wooden Box," Exploring Lassen County's Past, tipurdy.org.

Purdy, Tim. "Termo Post Office," Exploring Lassen County's Past, tipurdy.org, Aug. 7, 2017.

Purdy, Tim. "Those Bank of America Buildings," Exploring Lassen County's Past, tipurdy.org,
          April 22, 2017..

Purdy, Tim. "Wrede Hotel-Standish," Exploring Lassen County's Past, tipurdy.org, June 4, 2023.

Queenan, Charles F. "Remote Mining Town Stands Silent, Empty," Los Angeles Times, pt. VII, p. 2,
          May 1, 1988.

"Randsburg, California," westernmininghistory.com.

"The Randsburg City Jail," fotospot.com.

"Red Bluff-Susanville Road Now Closed," Napa Daily Register, p 4, Feb. 18, 1929.

Reed, Vivian. "Oasis of art in California desert/Owens Valley's unique light and landscape inspire
          creators, visitors," sfgate.com, Aug. 31, 2003.

"Riverside Hotel," renohistorical.org.

Roadside Architecture, roadarch.com.

Rocha, Guy. "Walley's Hot Springs not exactly the first," Geno Gazette-Journal, p. 19, Aug. 18, 2002.

Roe, Susan Marie Hillier. "A Childhood Hometown – Independence, Inyo County, California,"
          familyfoiblesandhistoryhangups.blogspot.com, Nov. 12, 2015.

"Rustic Oasis Motel," priceline.com.

"Sacramento Man Buys California Hotel in Alturas," Modoc County Record, p. 1, Sept. 18, 1952.

Sangree, Hudson. "Food on the Fly," latimes.com, May 5, 2002.

Sheehan, Bill. "The hungry hiker's roadside attractions," latimes.com, Oc. 14, 2003.

Shepardson, Mary. "Now and Then: A road runs through it," sandiegouniontribune.com, Aug. 5, 2016.

"The Slide Mountain Story Is Told Again As Proposal Is Made to Change Its Name,"
          Reno Evening Gazette,p. 2, April 5, 1952.

"SR-58 Kramer Junction Expressway," digital-desert.com.

"Surprise Valley Theater," cinematreasures.org

Takei, Barbara. "Tule Lake Preservation: A Progress Report," nichibei.org, Jan. 1, 2013.

"Tamarack Lodge," mammothtrails.org.

"This Small California Town is Regarded as One of the Most Haunted Places on Earth,"
          Travel Maven, May 16, 2023.

"Tioga Lodge at Mono Lake," sierranevadageotourism.org.

"Tioga Pass Road in Good Shape," San Francisco Chronicle, p. 2, July 18, 1920.

"Travel Over Three Flags Road Doubled," Alturas Plaindealer, p. 1, Sept. 18, 1935.

Twain, Mark. "Prize Fight in Washoe Valley: Fourteen Rounds Fought, Bloody Affray at the Close," Virginia City Territorial Enterprise, Sept. 23, 1863.

Twain, Mark. "Roughing It," American Publishing Company, Hartford, Conn., 1872.

"U.S. 395 History," floodgap.com.

"US 395, Part 6: Inyo and Mono Counties (Bishop to Mammoth)," floodgap.com.

"Victorville," route66times.com.

"Virginia Creek Settlement," tripadvisor.com.

"Wanderers Find Mono County is Worth Long Trip," Tulare Daily Advance, p. 4, Aug. 19, 1922.

"We Dare You To Take This Road Trip To Northern California's Most Abandoned Places," onlyinyourstate.com, March 8, 2017.

"Wheaton and Hollis Hotel and Bodie Store," bodie.com.

"The White Lady of the Bridgeport Inn," prairierosepublications.blogspot.com.

Williams, Michael J. "Lake Elsinore: Cultural Center's history celebrated," sandiegouniontribune.com, Dec. 2, 2011.

"Working Farm Roots: The Creation of Modoc National Wildlife Refuge," hmdb.org.

"Workmen Give Grand Central Finishing Touch," Reno Evening Gazette, p. 3, April 19, 1949.

Young, Gary. "Olancha was location in a 1960 Twilight Zone," kibskbov.com, Dec. 11, 2020.

Looking north to Mono Lake, with 395 on the lower and left side of the photo. *Author photo.*

About the author

Stephen H. Provost has written several books about life in 20th century America, including a dozen books on America's highways. During more than three decades in journalism, he has worked as a managing editor, copy desk chief, columnist, and reporter at five newspapers. Now a full-time author, he has written on such diverse topics as dragons, mutant superheroes, mythic archetypes, language, department stores, and his hometown. Visit him online and read his blogs at stephenhprovost.com.

Did you enjoy this book?

Recommend it to a friend. And please consider **rating it and/or leaving a brief review** at Amazon, Barnes & Noble, and Goodreads.

Also by the author

Works of Fiction

Crimson Scourge

The Memortality Saga

  Memortality

  Paralucidity

Academy of the Lost Labyrinth

  The Talismans of Time

  Pathfinder of Destiny

The Only Dragon

Identity Break

Nightmare's Eve

Feathercap

Works of Nonfiction

A Whole Different League

The Great American Shopping Experience

California's Historic Highways series

  Highway 99

  Highway 101

America's Historic Highways series

  America's First Highways

  Yesterday's Highways

  Highways of the South

Highways of the West series

  America's Loneliest Road

  Victory Road

  The Lincoln Highway in California (with Gary Kinst)

Roadside Illustrated series

  Happy Motoring!

  Signpost Up Ahead: The East

  Signpost Up Ahead: The West

Mark Twain's Nevada
The Century Cities series
  Cambria Century, Carson City Century
  Charleston Century, Danville Century
  Fresno Century, Goldfield Century
  Greensboro Century, Huntington Century
  Roanoke Century, San Luis Obispo Century
Fresno Growing Up
Martinsville Memories
The Legend of Molly Bolin
50 Undefeated
The Phoenix Chronicles
  The Osiris Testament
  The Way of the Phoenix
  The Gospel of the Phoenix
The Phoenix Principle
  Forged in Ancient Fires
  Messiah in the Making

All books available on Amazon

Use your phone's camera to scan the QR Code below

Praise for other works

"If you have any interest in highways, old diners and motels and such, or 20th century US history, this book is for you. It is without a doubt one of the best highway books ever published."
— Dan R. Young, Highway 101 historian, on **Yesterday's Highways**

"Both books are well-researched, nicely written, and illustrated with good black and white photographs, and both contribute importantly to highway literature."
— Wayne Shannon, *Jefferson Highway Declaration*,
on **Yesterday's Highways** and **America's First Highways**

"... an engaging narrative that pulls the reader into the story and onto the road. ... I highly recommend **Highway 99: The History of California's Main Street**, whether you're a roadside archaeology nut or just someone who enjoys a ripping story peppered with vintage photographs."
— Barbara Gossett,
Society for Commercial Archaeology Journal

"Profusely illustrated throughout, **Highway 99** is unreservedly recommended as an essential and core addition to every community and academic library's California History collections."
— California Bookwatch

"... it contains a lot of information I hadn't heard before. Both books prove well-written with few weaknesses..."
— Ron Warnick, route66news.com,
on **Yesterday's Highways** and **America's First Highways**

"An essential primer for anyone seeking an entrée into the genre. Provost serves up a smorgasbord of highlights gleaned from his personal memories of and research into the various nooks and crannies of what 'used-to-be' in professional team sports."
— Tim Hanlon, Good Seats Still Available,
on **A Whole Different League**

"As informed and informative as it is entertaining and absorbing, **Fresno Growing Up** is very highly recommended for personal, community, and academic library 20th Century
American History collections."

— John Burroughs, Reviewer's Bookwatch

"The complex idea of mixing morality and mortality is a fresh twist on the human condition. ... **Memortality** is one of those books that will incite more questions than it answers. And for fandom, that's a good thing."

— Ricky L. Brown, Amazing Stories

"Punchy and fast paced, **Memortality** reads like a graphic novel. ... (Provost's) style makes the trippy landscapes and mind-bending plot points more believable and adds a thrilling edge to this vivid crossover fantasy."

— Foreword Reviews

"The genres in this volume span horror, fantasy, and science-fiction, and each is handled deftly. ... **Nightmare's Eve** should be on your reading list. The stories are at the intersection of nightmare and lucid dreaming, up ahead a signpost ... next stop, your reading pile. Keep the nightlight on."

— R.B. Payne, Cemetery Dance

"**Memortality** by Stephen Provost is a highly original, thrilling novel unlike anything else out there."   — David
McAfee, bestselling author of

33 A.D., 61 A.D., and 79 A.D.

"Provost sticks mostly to the classics: vampires, ghosts, aliens, and even dragons. But trekking familiar terrain allows the author to subvert readers' expectations. ... Provost's poetry skillfully displays the same somber themes as the stories. ... Worthy tales that prove external forces are no more terrifying than what's inside people's heads."

— Kirkus Reviews on **Nightmare's Eve**

"The story feels so close, so intimate, we as readers experience the emotions, the events, and the conflicts, in what feels like real time. Gut-wrenchingly so."

— Stephen Mark Rainey, author of *Blue Devil Island*, on **Death's Doorstep**

SIERRA HIGHWAY

SIERRA HIGHWAY